Cambridge English
Compact
Advanced

Teacher's Book

Peter May

Cambridge University Press
www.cambridge.org/elt

Cambridge English Language Assessment
www.cambridgeenglish.org

Information on this title: www.cambridge.org/9781107418387

© Cambridge University Press and UCLES 2014

First published 2014

Printed in Dubai by Oriental Press

A catalogue record for this publication is available from the British Library

ISBN 978-1-107-41838-7 Teacher's Book
ISBN 978-1-107-41802-8 Student's Book with answers with CD-ROM
ISBN 978-1-107-41808-0 Student's Book without answers with CD-ROM
ISBN 978-1-107-41828-8 Class Audio CDs (2)
ISBN 978-1-107-41782-3 Workbook without answers with Audio
ISBN 978-1-107-41790-8 Workbook with answers with Audio
ISBN 978-1-107-41819-6 Student's Book Pack (Student's Book with answers with CD-ROM and Class Audios (2))
ISBN 978-1-107-41831-8 Presentation Plus DVD-ROM
ISBN 978-1-107-41832-5 Interactive ebook: Student's Book with answers
ISBN 978-1-107-41794-6 Interactive ebook: Workbook with answers

Additional resources for this publication at www.cambridge.org/compactadvanced

Produced by Wild Apple

Contents

Map of the units

	TOPICS	GRAMMAR	VOCABULARY
1	Events, issues & the media	Review of past, present & future tenses	Collocations Frequently confused words
2	Travel, customs & traditions	Participle clauses	Prefixes Academic expressions
3	Human behaviour & relationships	Review of reported speech	Collocations Idioms with *keep*
4	Money & business	Review of passive forms Causatives	Fixed phrases Phrasal verbs with *out* Money vocabulary
5	Health & sport	Conditionals including mixed forms & forms without *if*	Word building Suffixes Compound adjectives
6	The arts & entertainment	Review of verbs + *-ing* or infinitive	Collocations Frequently confused words
7	Nature & the environment	Inversion after negative adverbials	Collocations Phrasal verbs with *on* Idioms: nature
8	Education, learning & work	Relative clauses Introductory *it/what*	Affixes Spelling changes
9	Science & technology	Modals, including continuous & passive forms	Dependent prepositions Science lexis
10	Psychology & personality	Wishes & regrets	Three-part phrasal verbs Adjectives of personality

READING AND USE OF ENGLISH	WRITING	LISTENING	SPEAKING
Part 1: multiple-choice cloze Part 7: gapped text	Part 1 essay: get ideas, contrast links, checking	Part 4: multiple matching	Part 1: talking about past, present & future
Part 3: word formation Part 6: cross-text multiple matching	Part 2 report: planning, recommending	Part 2: sentence completion	Part 2: making comparisons
Part 4: key word transformations Part 5: multiple-choice questions	Part 2 letter: formal / informal / neutral style; layout	Part 1: short texts, multiple-choice questions	Part 3: suggesting, (dis)agreeing, asking for opinions
Part 2: open cloze Part 7: gapped text	Part 1 essay: addition links, achieving balance	Part 3: long text, multiple-choice questions	Part 4: expressing & justifying opinions
Part 3: word formation Part 8: multiple matching	Part 2 proposal: purpose links, text organisation	Part 2: sentence completion	Part 2: commenting on partner's pictures
Part 1: multiple-choice cloze Part 5: multiple-choice questions	Part 2 review: praising & criticising	Part 4: multiple matching	Part 1: expressing preferences, likes & dislikes
Part 4: key word transformations Part 7: gapped text	Part 1 essay: sentence adverbs, paraphrasing notes	Part 1: short texts, multiple-choice questions	Part 3: giving examples, helping your partner
Part 3: word formation Part 8: multiple matching	Part 2 letter: formal language, text organisation	Part 2: sentence completion	Part 4: adding emphasis, hedging
Part 2: open cloze Part 5: multiple-choice questions	Part 2 report: result links, text organisation	Part 3: long text, multiple-choice questions	Part 2: speculating about present & past
Part 4: key word transformations Part 6: cross-text multiple matching	Part 1: concession, opening paragraphs	Part 4: multiple matching	Parts 3 & 4: negotiating, reaching a decision

Introduction

Who *Compact Advanced* is for

Compact Advanced is a short but highly intensive final preparation course for students planning to take the revised *Cambridge English: Advanced* exam from Cambridge English Language Assessment. It provides C1-level students with thorough preparation and practice of the grammar, vocabulary, language skills and exam skills needed for success. The course is particularly suitable for students of 16 and over.

What the Student's Book contains

- *Compact Advanced* Student's Book has ten units for classroom study. Each unit covers practice in Reading and Use of English, Writing, Listening and Speaking. Interesting Reading and Listening texts cover topics that may appear in the *Cambridge English: Advanced (CAE)* exam. Writing tasks include both sample and model answers and follow a step-by-step approach. The Speaking activities are designed to improve fluency and accuracy, and to help students express themselves with confidence.

- Grammar pages provide additional focus on advanced-level grammar. Vocabulary input is at C1-level and is based on the English Vocabulary Profile. Grammar and vocabulary work is integrated in exam practice, including exercises based on research from the Cambridge Learner Corpus.

- *Quick steps* give advice on how to approach each exam task type.

- *Exam tips* give useful advice on exam strategies.

- All units include cross references to the Writing and Speaking Guides, and Grammar reference.

Writing and Speaking guides

These guides explain in detail what students can expect in Writing and Speaking and give suggestions on how best to prepare and practise in each case. The guides include a summary of the strategies, advice and tips focused on in the units of the Student's Book, with additional tasks and model answers in the Writing guide, and lists of useful expressions in the Speaking guide.

The **Grammar reference** gives clear explanations of all the main areas of grammar students need to know for *Cambridge English: Advanced (CAE)*.

Wordlist

The wordlist includes approximately 30 key words with definitions for each unit.

CD-ROM

The CD-ROM accompanying the Student's Book contains interactive grammar, vocabulary and writing practice activities as well as an electronic version of the wordlist, and a link to the *Online Cambridge Advanced Learner's Dictionary*.

Student's Book with answers

This component includes all the answer keys and recording scripts for the Student's Book.

Other course components

Two audio CDs contain listening material for the ten units of the Student's Book. The icon used with listening activities indicates the CD and track numbers.

Teacher's Book including:

- A list of aims for each unit.

- Step-by-step guidance for presenting and teaching all the material in the Student's Book. In some cases, alternative treatments and extension activities are suggested.

- Complete answer keys with recording scripts for the Student's Book. The keys include sample and model answers for Writing tasks.

- Photocopiable recording scripts.

- Five photocopiable progress tests with answer keys, one for every two Student's Book units. The tests use a variety of non-exam task types.

Workbook without answers with Audio including:

- Ten units for homework and self-study corresponding to the Student's Book units. Each unit has four pages of exercises providing further practice and consolidation of the language and exam skills presented in the Student's Book. Exercises are based on research from the Cambridge Learner Corpus. Vocabulary is based on the English Vocabulary Profile.

Workbook with answers with Audio includes all the answer keys and recording scripts for the Workbook.

Additional resources for this publication can be found at www.cambridge.org/compactadvanced

Cambridge English: Advanced

Reading and Use of English 1 hour 30 minutes

Parts 1 and 3 mainly test your vocabulary; Part 2 mainly tests grammar. Part 4 often tests both vocabulary and grammar. Parts 5–8 test reading comprehension.

Part	Task type	Questions	Format
1	Multiple-choice cloze	8	Fill each gap in a text from options A, B, C or D.
2	Open cloze	8	Fill each gap in a text with one word.
3	Word formation	8	Fill each gap in a text with the right form of a given word.
4	Key word transformation	6	Complete a sentence with a given word and up to five more words to mean the same as another sentence.
5	Multiple choice	6	Read a text followed by questions with four options: A, B, C or D.
6	Cross-text multiple matching	4	Read across four short texts and match prompts to the correct sections.
7	Gapped text	6	Read a text with six paragraphs removed. There are seven paragraphs to choose from.
8	Multiple matching	10	Read one or more texts. Match prompts to elements in the texts.

Writing 90 minutes

You have to do Part 1 plus one of the Part 2 tasks. In Part 2 you can choose one of questions 2–4.

Part	Task type	Words	Format
1	discursive essay	220–260	Write in response to two points given in an input text. Give reasons for your opinion.
2	letter / email, proposal, report or review	220–260	Choose one from three tasks based on a given context and topic, with a clear purpose and target reader

Listening about 40 minutes

You both hear and see the instructions for each task, and you hear all four parts twice.

Part	Task type	Questions	Format
1	Multiple choice	6	Three short extracts with one or two people talking for about a minute in three different situations. For each of two questions, you choose from answers A, B or C.
2	Sentence completion	8	One person speaking for about three minutes. Complete sentences by writing a word or short phrase.
3	Multiple choice	6	An interview or conversation of about four minutes. Choose from answers A, B, C or D.
4	Multiple matching	10	Five extracts of about 30 seconds each, with a common theme. For each extract there are two tasks. Choose from a list of eight possible answers.

Speaking 15 minutes

You do the Speaking test with one other candidate. There are two examiners, but one of them does not take part in the conversation.

Part	Task type	Minutes	Format
1	The examiner asks you questions.	2	Talk about yourself.
2	Talk on your own for one minute.	4	Talk about two pictures and then comment on the other candidate's pictures for about 30 seconds.
3	Talk to your partner.	4	A two-minute discussion. You then have a minute to make a decision.
4	Discuss topics connected with the theme of Part 3.	5	A discussion led by the examiner.

1 Breaking news

Unit objectives

TOPICS	events, issues and the media
GRAMMAR	review of past, present & future tenses
VOCABULARY	collocations; frequently confused words
READING AND USE OF ENGLISH	Part 1: multiple choice cloze; Part 7: gapped text
WRITING	Part 1 essay: get ideas, contrast links, checking
LISTENING	Part 4: multiple matching
SPEAKING	Part 1: talking about past, present & future

Listening

Part 4

1 Students work in pairs. Check they have labelled the pictures correctly and then allow a few minutes for brief discussion of the issues raised by the questions. Point out that the adjectives are all C1 level, or derived from C1 words.

> **Suggested answers**
>
> 1 The meteorite strike (D) and the volcanic eruption (B) are clearly natural and the oil spill (A) is almost certainly man-made, but although the wildfire (C) might be caused by lightning, it is usually started accidentally or on purpose by people. It could also be partly the result of man-made global warming and drought.
> 2 Student answers will vary from country to country, but it may depend on the amount and quality of film available, the number of casualties, the harm to the environment and – in the case of the oil spill – criticism of large companies.

2 Begin by pointing out that this task type is different from those they may already be familiar with from lower-level exams, in that they will have to carry out two tasks either at the same time or in sequence. Allow a minute for pairs to look at the task and questions, then elicit the answers. Make sure everyone has the correct answers and take any further questions they may have on Listening Part 4.

> **Answers**
>
> 1 five   2 In Task One, listen for which event each speaker is talking about; in Task Two, listen for what surprised each speaker most about the event   3 three

3 Give pairs a couple of minutes to do this, then check. Point out there are no right or wrong answers – different people will suggest different words in both cases.

Suggested answers

Task One: A ground, shaking, trembling   B sea, pollution, sticky   C wind, blow, speed   D burn, trees, bushes   E lava, throw, flow   F space, speed, impact   G water, soak, boat   H twist, lift, dark

Task Two: A number, injured (victims, casualties, hurt)
B cause (explain, result, consequence)
C decrease, speed (slow down, move, decelerate)
D direction (course, head, destination)
E extent, damage (how much, scale, destroy)
F lack, noise (sound, quiet, silence)
G where (location, spot, centred)
H number, unreported (quantity, no news, ignored)

4 🔘 *1.02* Refer the class to the Quick steps and the Exam tip, then play the recording right through, in exam conditions, without pausing. When it has finished, allow a few seconds for the class to check they have put an answer to every question and then go through the answers.

If you wish, photocopy the script on page 69 for the students and ask them to underline the sections which give the answers.

Exam task

> **Answers**
>
> 1 H   2 D   3 B   4 A   5 G   6 F   7 D   8 H   9 B   10 E

> **Recording script**
>
> *Part 4 consists of two tasks. You'll hear five short extracts in which people are talking about unusual events they witnessed. Look at Task 1. For questions 1–5, choose from the list (A–H) the event each speaker is talking about. Now look at Task 2. For questions 6–10, choose from the list (A–H) what surprised each speaker most about the event. While you listen you must complete both tasks.*
>
> *You now have 45 seconds to look at Part 4.*
>
> *Speaker 1*
>
> As I looked across the countryside, (1) I saw that distinctive shape sweeping across the distant fields and then over the surface of the lake which at that time of the year was of course full. There it picked up huge quantities of water and then continued overland on its way. It could have gone in any direction, but I'd had a strange feeling that it was coming after me and sure enough it kept on heading my way, closer and closer. I'd been expecting it to make a really deafening sound but (6) what struck me was the way it twisted across the open flat farmland in virtual silence, and somehow that made it even more alarming.

Speaker 2

It was when I reached a point overlooking the valley that I saw it gradually moving east far below me, consuming everything in its path as such intense ones always do. It was quite a scary sight, though when I thought about it rationally (7) it seemed highly unlikely it would suddenly alter course and put me in danger. But when it reached the bushes at the foot of the hill where I was standing, that was exactly what happened. (2) Fuelled by the dry vegetation on the steep slope, it began racing towards me and I fled back down the way I'd come to safety. Later I was told they tend to accelerate when they spread uphill, on other occasions reaching homes on higher ground with tragic results.

Speaker 3

I suppose I should have been shocked when I saw for myself just how many square miles it covered, and (3) how dense were the clouds of smoke where attempts were being made to burn it off, but having previously studied satellite photos I knew pretty much what to expect. I still, though, felt deep sadness at the immense harm that sticky mess was causing to wildlife, both above and beneath the surface. That feeling wasn't helped by my travelling companion reminding me of the depressing statistics in such cases, but (8) what really shook me was the figure he quoted for the frequency of such disasters, the majority of which the media are either unaware of or choose to ignore. Apparently it runs into dozens, every month.

Speaker 4

My friend Lauren and I were out walking in the hills on a hot, sunny day when we noticed (4) a kind of trembling under our feet, rather like when you're standing on a bridge and a lorry goes past. But there were no vehicles in sight, no road or rail tunnels below us – and the nearest volcano was half a continent away. Then Lauren said she'd seen a local press report about an oil company pumping liquid underground to extract oil and gas, which caused huge sections of the rock to suddenly shift below that part of the countryside. (9) So that was the explanation, as apparently even the really major ones can be pretty quiet. I was speechless.

Speaker 5

I'd heard warnings on the radio so I was half-expecting something like this to happen here, but (10) destruction on this kind of scale was not something I'd envisaged. Trapped on the roof, I surveyed the dreadful scene around me. Local landmarks such as the flower gardens were unrecognisable, and when eventually they reappeared they would be covered in thick black mud. Much worse, though, would be the effect on people's homes, where (5) possessions would be soaked and ruined. Other houses were burning, no doubt because of electrical appliances left switched on. I did spot two firefighters rowing along a street, but their priority was to take the very young and the very old to safety, not to try to put out fires.

See the Workbook and CD-ROM for further practice.

Grammar

Review of verb tenses

1 Give pairs plenty of time to look at and discuss these sentences. Elicit the names of all the tenses and advise them to check the Grammar reference, page 88. Go through the answers with the class, eliciting more examples of the less common tenses, such as the future perfect, future perfect continuous or past perfect continuous.

Answers

1 a) I see them at weekends/every weekend – a habit. (Present simple)
   b) I'm seeing them next weekend – an arrangement. (Present continuous)
2 a) The theme tune began immediately after the end of the programme. (Past simple)
   b) The theme tune had already begun before the programme ended. (Past perfect)
3 a) They had started taking photos before Melanie walked in (probably of other people), and continued doing so. (Past continuous)
   b) They started taking photos (of Melanie) when she walked in. (Past simple)
4 a) We'll start watching the film before you get here. (Future continuous)
   b) We'll wait until you arrive before we start watching that film. (Future simple)
5 a) At some time in her life, she has written that book. (Present perfect)
   b) She is still writing that book, or has just finished writing it. (Present perfect continuous)
6 a) When our plane takes off, the thunderstorm will be over. (Future perfect)
   b) When our plane takes off, there will still be a thunderstorm but it will be nearly over. (Future continuous)
7 a) The change in government policy led to rapid growth. (Past simple)
   b) Rapid growth ended when the government policy changed. (Past perfect continuous)
8 a) I'll start working abroad when I'm 25 and continue for several years. (Future simple)
   b) I have already started or will start working abroad several years before I'm 25. (Future perfect continuous)

2 Point out that although some of these mistakes may seem rather basic, they were all made by *Cambridge English: Advanced* candidates. Go through the answers with the class, asking why they think each mistake was made.

Answers

1 Do you come → Are you coming / Will you be coming / Are you going to come (simple present not used for future plans)
2 I'm waiting → I'll be waiting (future continuous for a background action)
3 know → have known (present perfect needed with *for* + time reference, showing something started in the past and still continues)
4 send → am sending / am going to send (present continuous for current action/writing convention)
5 was waiting → had been waiting (past perfect continuous for a past action continuing up to another past action)
6 you'll come → you come (present simple after future time markers such *as when, as soon as*)
7 arranged → had arranged (the arrangement was made before the meeting, so it has to be past perfect)
8 are needing → need / will need / are going to need (*need* is a state verb with no continuous form)

3 Explain that only one of the three possible answers is correct in each case. Give individuals or pairs a few minutes to do this, and then check. Focus on any particular difficulties that may emerge. You may also want to practise the pronunciation of the contracted forms.

4 Put the class into new pairs, so that everyone has the chance to tell someone they don't know very well about themselves. Point out that they can mark any year on the timeline, not just 2000, 2005, etc. If necessary, prompt with more life events, e.g. moving house, making new friends, learning a new skill. Monitor pairs for accuracy, and at the end elicit some of the answers as a class activity.

Suggested answers

2000: started primary school. I was living in the city centre; I used to walk to school.
2005: started secondary school. I'd learned to swim before then; I'd been studying English for two years by then.
2012: left school. I've made new friends since then; I've been studying at university since then.

5 In the same pairs, students tell each other about their future hopes and dreams.

Suggested answers

2016: will graduate. I'll be living in another city then.
2017: will get a job. I'll have travelled around the world by then.
2022: will buy a flat. I'll have been saving for five years by then.

See the Workbook and CD-ROM for further practice.

Reading and Use of English

Part 7

1 Put the class into pairs and make sure everyone understands the questions, especially 'paywall', which will appear in the exam task text. When they are working, be ready to help with any semi-technical words they may need, such as *scroll, tablet* or *e-reader*.

If this task type is new to your students, begin by telling them to look at the instructions and the options A–G. Then they answer these questions:

1 What is the topic of the text? (online versions of printed publications)

2 What must you put in gaps 1–7? (six missing paragraphs)

3 Do you need to use all of paragraphs A–G? (no – one is not needed (but they will have to find out which))

Give the class a minute to look at the task, then elicit the answers.

Answers

Students' own answers

2 Allow three minutes, at most, for this initial reading task, then go through the answers.

Answers

Sales of news & current affairs magazines, and worldwide sales of printed newspapers have been rising. Sales of printed books and European printed newspapers, as well as online advertising in newspapers have been falling.

3 Explain that there will nearly always be language links between the paragraphs in the main text and options A–G. Elicit the answers to question 1 from the class and then give pairs a few minutes to do 2. Tell them that in this exercise they should focus on just the first sentence of each paragraph, in some cases finding more than one expression, but that in future Part 7 exercises they may also need to find links in other parts of paragraphs, particularly at the end.

Elicit other common reference words and contrast links such as *them, her, however* and *on the other hand* and tell the class to look out for these in gapped text exercises.

Answers

1 reference words and phrases, contrast links
2 1 *all of which* refers back to a number of assertions in the missing paragraph.
2 *As for* indicates a further example, with the previous example(s) in the missing paragraph.
3 *Yet* introduces a contrast with information in the missing paragraph.
A *In other words* introduces an explanation of a point in the missing paragraph.
B *these* refer back to *tales* of this kind previously mentioned (in fact they aren't: it is the distractor).
C *Such* adds emphasis to *varying national trends* described in the missing paragraph.
3 4 And even 5 Already 6 this D One E But, it
F similar G So, that, so little

4 Refer the class to the Quick steps and the Exam tip, then tell them to do this on their own. Allow just 12–15 minutes, as they have already read the text for gist and located some of the language clues. At the end, remind them to check they have put an answer to every question, then go through the answers.

Exam task

Answers

1 E **2** D **3** F **4** G **5** C **6** A; not needed: B

Reading and Use of English

Part 1

Collocations

1 Begin by explaining that collocations are words that often go together, and give a few examples, e.g. *offer, take* or *give* advice, but not *make* or *do* advice. Explain that this exercise focuses on verb + noun collocations, but other combinations are also common. Tell pairs they can use their dictionaries for this activity, pointing out that entries may include common collocations. Check their answers.

2 Remind the class that the fact several words may collocate
with another does not necessarily indicate they have the
same, or even similar, meanings, and that they may also
go with different structures. Give pairs a few minutes to
complete the sentences, then elicit the answers and any
alternatives.

Answers

1 edit **2** submit **3** broadcast **4** scheduled **5** draft
6 research **7** covering **8** carrying, running, putting,
publishing, reporting, featuring, covering

3 Focus attention on the first Quick step, pointing out that
their first aim is to get a general idea of what the text about.
Allow only a minute for reading, then elicit the answer.

Answers

Only if they ask people's permission first, and pay them for their
material.

4 Tell the class always to look at the example in multiple-
choice cloze. Give pairs a minute to study the first sentence
of the text and item 0, then elicit the answer. Remind
the class that collocations are not necessarily formed
by adjoining words, and that they may be formed by
more than two words. Point out that in this case the verb
collocates both with *event* and *camera*, which gives *capture*
a figurative meaning here. Ask the class to think of another
verb used in this way *(shoot)*.

Answers

events

5 Point out that although half the missing words are verbs
and the rest are nouns, all collocate with nouns. Allow a
few minutes for pairs to do the collocation exercise. If you
check their answers before they proceed, it will make the
exam task a little easier. Alternatively, you may prefer to
leave checking until after they have finished the exam task.
When they have finished that, go through the answers. You
may want to highlight other vocabulary items both in the
text and among the options, many of which are useful C1-
level words.

Answers

1 social **2** images **3** images/on social media
4 (public) interest **5** research **6** role **7** steps **8** permission

See the Workbook and CD-ROM for further practice.

Exam task

Read through the Exam tip with the class before they begin.

Answers

1 A **2** B **3** D **4** B **5** A **6** C **7** D **8** B

6 Give pairs several minutes to discuss these topics, all of
which arise from the exam text. Encourage the use of
collocations from Exercise 1.

Speaking

Frequently confused words

1 Give pairs several minutes to do this, using dictionaries
to distinguish between the alternatives and/or check the
various forms of verbs such as *rise/raise*. Go through the
answers, and if time allows elicit more words that can cause
difficulties. Depending on their first language(s), these
might include false cognates such as *adequate/suitable*,
actual/present, *kind/sympathetic* or *remark/notice*.

Answers

1 sensitive **2** brought up **3** implies **4** risen **5** attend
6 economical **7** lay **8** opportunity

See the CD-ROM for further practice.

Part 1

2 Refer the class to the illustration. You may want to ask the
class if they have done such a Speaking test before, e.g.
at First level, and arrange pairs so that one at least has
experience of this kind of test. Give them a few minutes
to discuss the statements, then go through the answers,
eliciting reasons and more information where appropriate.
Page 107 of the Speaking guide will give them some further
information.

Answers

1 True, though it may be a little longer if there are three
candidates.
2 True, the other is the Assessor.
3 False, questions are asked of each individual.
4 False, though candidates should be polite at all times.
5 False. It would sound unnatural and the examiners would not
allow it.
6 True. If candidates don't know the exact words – or
remember the exact details – to give completely honest
answers, they can make them up.

3 Quickly elicit the answers and point out that the class will
hear these questions in the recording to follow.

Suggested answers

1 present simple; possibly also present perfect, past
simple **2** present simple; possibly also present
continuous **3** future continuous; possibly also future perfect
4 present simple; future **5** present simple
6 present simple **7** 2nd conditional

4 ⊙ *1.03* Remind the class that the format of Part 1 means
they will be able to concentrate on listening to one speaker
at a time, and play the recording twice. They note down
Y, N or P for each speaker in categories 1–5 as they listen.
(*Possibly* meaning there isn't quite enough information to
judge.) Afterwards, elicit the choice of answers and ask a
few students to give reasons.

If you wish, photocopy the script on page 70 for students to check their answers.

Suggested answers

Cristina **1** Y   **2** Y   **3** Y   **4** Y   **5** Y
Markus **1** Y   **2** P   **3** N   **4** P   **5** N

Recording script

Teacher: OK, Cristina. Where are you from?

Cristina: I'm from Getafe, which is quite a big town about ten kilometres to the south of Madrid.

Teacher: What do you do there?

Cristina: I'm a student. I've been studying information technology at the university of Móstoles since about two years ago.

Teacher: What do you think you'll be doing in five years' time?

Cristina: Can you repeat that, please?

Teacher: What do you think you'll be doing in five years' time?

Cristina: Er, it's hard to say, really, but I hope very much I'll be working in a big company. Maybe abroad because it is very difficult to find a job in Spain, even with a degree.

Teacher: How important do you think it is to speak more than one language?

Cristina: It's definitely very important, especially English. And if you speak both Spanish and English you can have many opportunities in the future, in the western part of the world anyway.

Teacher: OK, Markus. Where are you from?

Markus: I grew up in Hamburg.

Teacher: What do you most enjoy about learning English?

Markus: The grammar. It is relatively simple, I think.

Teacher: Do you prefer to get the news from television, newspapers or the Internet?

Markus: The Internet.

Teacher: Why?

Markus: You can compare, er, sources of news. In many cases, they report the same story in completely different ways.

Teacher: What would you do if you suddenly became very rich?

Markus: I would buy a house. I'd like to have an extremely large garden.

---

5 🔘 *1.04* Play Markus' part again. Begin by eliciting some general comments on Markus' speaking, and encourage the class to suggest ways he could have expanded his answers, as well as using the introductory expressions given. Do this orally as a class activity. Students can work in pairs to make the necessary changes. They don't have to use all the expressions.

Recording script

Teacher: OK, Markus. Where are you from?

Markus: I grew up in Hamburg.

Teacher: What do you most enjoy about learning English?

Markus: The grammar. It is relatively simple, I think.

Teacher: Do you prefer to get the news from television, newspapers or the Internet?

Markus: The Internet.

Teacher: Why?

Markus: You can compare, er, sources of news. In many cases, they report the same story in completely different ways.

Teacher: What would you do if you suddenly became very rich?

Markus: I would buy a house. I'd like to have an extremely large garden.

✳ **Suggested answers**

Well, as a matter of fact I grew up in Hamburg, which is a big port city in northern Germany.
That's not an easy question to answer, but perhaps the grammar. It is relatively simple, I think, at least compared to German grammar.
I suppose nowadays it's mainly from the Internet, like most people.
You can compare sources of news because in many cases they report the same story in completely different ways, depending on their political point of view.
I've never really thought about that before, but I imagine I would buy a house. And if possible I'd like it to have an extremely large garden, with a wide variety of trees and plants.

6 Focus attention on the Quick steps and the Exam tip. Explain to the 'examiners' that they should ask each 'candidate' four or five questions in sequence, then do the same – though asking different questions – with the other candidate. Tell candidates to use expressions from Exercise 5 and to be careful with verb tenses and the words from Exercise 1. Get everyone to start at the same time and time them to ensure that each dialogue lasts about a minute. When they comment on each other's performance, remind them to give praise as well as polite, constructive criticism. Suggest they highlight any difficulties with tenses.

Writing

Contrast links

1 Let pairs do these and then elicit the answers. Highlight some of the vocabulary, e.g. *a generation ago*, *discrimination*, *by law*, *region*, which they may find useful later on.

Answers

1 whereas; while   **2** Whereas; Although   **3** Despite the fact that; Even though   **4** In contrast; However   **5** Contrary to; In spite of   **6** Nevertheless; Despite this   **7** In spite of the fact that; Though   **8** Conversely; On the other hand

---

See the Workbook for further practice.

---

2 This exercise both practises the structures following the different linking expressions and provides preparation for the kinds of sentence transformation they may need to do in Reading and Use of English Part 3 (see Unit 3). Tell the class to do these on their own, then go through the answers.

Answers

1 many ordinary criminals have been released, political prisoners remain in jail.
2 though health care has improved, it is still not up to international standards.
3 of the fact that unemployment has fallen / of the fall in unemployment, the number of homeless people has risen.
4 the workers' income is increasing, (but) on the other hand their quality of life is going down.
5 (that) that country produces a lot of food, ordinary people have little to eat.
6 to what some people say, we don't spend enough on overseas aid.
7 fruit prices have risen, farmers are getting paid less.
8 they/it ban(s) all opposition.

3 Begin by eliciting the issues shown in the photos (the gap between rich and poor). Encourage students to try to use the contrast links in Exercise 1, e.g. *Whereas the people in the first photo obviously have plenty of money, those in the second photo can't even afford to buy their own food.*

For extra practice, give students the following points to compare in pairs:

- 'traditional' male jobs / 'traditional' female jobs

- child labour / children at school

- over-eating / famine

- excessive water use / drought

- city-centre housing / housing in affluent suburbs

Monitor as they are speaking. If time allows, discuss each issue briefly as a class, bearing in mind that the essay task below will focus on some aspects of them. Then tell individuals to write at least one, preferably two, pairs of sentences about each issue. They can compare their sentences with a partner. Check their work for accuracy.

Suggested answers

Even though there have been some changes in society, men still tend to have better-paid jobs than women.
Despite the fact that education is a universal human right, many children still have to work instead of going to school.
People in some countries eat more than they need. In contrast, other people in the world are starving.
In some parts of the world people waste fresh water, while elsewhere there isn't enough for crops, or even to drink.
People in the city centre often live in crowded conditions, whereas those in well-off parts of town have big houses with gardens.

Part 1: essay

4 Writing Part 1 instructions are quite long and it may be the first time some students have seen this task type, so give pairs plenty of time to study the instructions, notes and comments.

When they have finished, go through the answers with the class, taking any other questions they may have on Part 1.

Answers

1 You have to write about ways people in richer countries can become more aware of poverty / raising awareness of poverty as a global issue. You are writing for your tutor.
2 You must write about any two of the notes, i.e. education, campaigns by charities, increased media coverage.
3 You can include one or more of the three opinions expressed. You shouldn't use exactly the same words in your essay.

5 Give pairs several minutes to study the model essay and note down their answers. Go through these with the class, taking any vocabulary questions they may have.

Answers

1 1st paragraph
2 increased media coverage, 2nd paragraph; education, 3rd paragraph
3 1st opinion in 3rd paragraph (*attention should also…*), 3rd opinion in 2nd paragraph (*Regular in-depth reports…*)
4 increased media coverage, 4th paragraph. She thinks education would be too slow and not affect older people; also, everyone takes notice of the media.
5 Yes it is. It's fairly formal.
6 despite, however, although, nevertheless, whereas

6 Students do this brainstorming activity in pairs or small groups before writing their essay individually. They should make notes as they discuss. You may want to elicit some answers to Question 1 only. Suggest they ask themselves similar questions about the topic whenever they tackle a Part 1 task.

7 Allow students, working on their own, three or four minutes to do this. Read through the Exam tip with the class and suggest they also note down in their plan some contrast links and vocabulary they could use.

8 Ideally, try to plan for students to write this essay in class. Give them 35-40 minutes to write and check their work (they normally have 45 minutes but they have already planned it). This includes two or three minutes to check their own work. Remind them that they should always do this in the exam. Alternatively, this could be done as a peer correction activity, giving pairs a few minutes to make suggestions about each other's work and for them to make any necessary changes. If you do not have time in class, ask students to write the essay for homework, noting down their start and finish times. They should aim to write it within the given time. Refer students to page 99 of the Writing guide for further information.

See the Workbook for further practice.

Travels and traditions

Unit objectives

TOPICS	travel, customs & traditions
GRAMMAR	participle clauses
VOCABULARY	prefixes; academic expressions
READING AND	Part 3: word formation;
USE OF ENGLISH	Part 6: cross-text multiple matching
WRITING	Part 2 report: planning, recommending
LISTENING	Part 2: sentence completion
SPEAKING	Part 2: making comparisons

Reading and Use of English

Part 6

1 Give pairs a few minutes to discuss these, then ask the class for their suggestions of their top three, with reasons.

2 Explain that this is the topic of the exam task text, and elicit the meaning of *gap year* in question 5. (The term is used in the exam task text. It is the year between leaving school and starting university that is usually spent travelling or working.) Give pairs three or four minutes to discuss these points, but don't elicit any answers.

3 Students may not have seen this task type before, so allow a couple of minutes for pairs to familiarise themselves with it and answer the questions. Go through the answers to these, and to any other questions they may have about the task.

> **Answers**
>
> **1** No   **2** They all relate to the same topic, in this case international volunteering.   **3** formal, academic   **4** attitude and opinion   **5** attitudes and opinions expressed in more than one text

4 Give pairs a couple of minutes to read and another two or three minutes to discuss. Don't elicit the answers.

5 Point out that in Part 6, candidates sometimes have to deal with difficult vocabulary, often by finding clues in the context. Focus, for instance, on *altruism* on line 14 in text A, which is followed by an explanation of its meaning. Tell students to do this activity on their own, then quickly go through the answers, without taking other questions on the text.

> **Answers**
>
> **1** although – whilst   **2** small and unimportant – negligible   **3** for this reason – hence   **4** mention without talking about directly – allude to   **5** caused to behave in a particular way – motivated   **6** in a morally correct way – ethically   **7** improved – enhanced   **8** description of a situation – scenario   **9** a sign of something (bad) – symptomatic   **10** written or spoken communication – discourse

6 Read the Exam tip with the class. Then give them, working individually, about 15 minutes to do the underlining and the exam task. Check the answers to both when they have finished, and focus on any difficulties they had with the task and/or the texts.

> **Answers**
>
> **2** different, others, why, work   **3** same, A, long-term effects, volunteers   **4** shares, C, who, volunteers

Exam task

> **Answers**
>
> **1** D   **2** D   **3** C   **4** B

> See the Workbook and CD-ROM for further practice.

Grammar

Participle clauses

1 Refer the class to the Grammar reference on page 89 and allow plenty of time for them to do the exercise. Point out that in some cases more than one answer is possible. When they have finished, check their answers for accuracy and then elicit more examples of each of these types of participle clause.

> **Suggested answers**
>
> **1g** We eventually stopped for a rest because we were feeling tired. / Because we were feeling tired, we eventually stopped for a rest.
> **2h** A lion approached. It was looking / It looked hungry.
> **3b** In order not to take any chances, they kept away from the cliff edge. / They kept away from the cliff edge in order not to take any chances.
> **4f** As soon as Carlos noticed the huge hole in the road, he hit the brakes. / Carlos hit the brakes as soon as he noticed the huge hole in the road.
> **5d** We bought our tickets and then we boarded the ferry.
> **6a** As long as they are handled carefully, those creatures are not dangerous. / Those creatures are not dangerous as long as they are handled carefully.
> **7c** The bridge collapsed, so we were (left) stranded on the island.
> **8e** The Atacama, which is the world's driest desert, is located in Chile and Peru. / The Atacama, which is located in Chile and Peru, is the world's driest desert.

2 Go over the first example as a class. Explain that the participle clause always relates to the subject of the main clause, and the sentence can sound strange if this is not the case, e.g. *Driving through the countryside, the mountains came into view.* (So, the mountains are driving!) You may (or may not) want to tell the class that these are sometimes called 'dangling participles'. It is quite a fun exercise so let students work in pairs to complete the exercise before checking as a class.

Answers

1 It appears that we, the readers, are driven crazy with thirst. *Suggested answer:* We read how the crew, driven crazy with thirst, survive in an open boat.
2 It sounds as though Sean was barking. *Suggested answer:* Barking loudly, a large dog approached Sean.
3 It sounds as though the speaker has been washed. *Suggested answer:* After being washed in hot water, my clothes had turned pink, I noticed.
4 It implies that tall buildings are scared of heights. *Suggested answer:* Scared of heights, Joey avoids tall buildings.
5 It indicates that both Tanya and I finished my breakfast. *Suggested answer:* Having finished my breakfast, I set off on foot with Tanya.
6 It implies the footpath does not wish to damage the plants. *Suggested answer:* Not wishing to damage the plants, walkers use the footpath.
7 It appears you are watered every day. *Suggested answer:* Watered every day, these plants grow quickly, you will find.
8 It appears the ticket was running. *Suggested answer:* Running to catch the train, I dropped my ticket onto the platform.

3 Students could do this exercise individually before checking their answers in pairs. Encourage them to try out these structures when they are doing writing tasks in English – the examiners reward more complex sentences if they are accurately written.

Answers

1 Looking tired, Marta said she had been travelling all night.
2 Climbing in the mountains, we saw an eagle fly past.
3 Worn with matching trousers, this jacket looks great.
4 Being tall, Joaquin could see over the crowd's heads.
5 Exhausted by the journey, I slept for 18 hours.
6 Our vehicle broke down, leaving us stuck in the forest.
7 Having studied Mandarin for five years, my sister speaks it well.
8 Not having anyone to talk to, Jack felt lonely.

4 Students need to read the text through before starting the exercise. You could ask one of them to read it aloud to the class. Tell students to do this on their own, and suggest that when they have drafted pieces of writing in the future they may want to make some similar changes to their texts to achieve a greater variety of structures. Elicit the answers – and possible variations – when everyone has finished. Remind them to write their answers with the correct punctuation. Point out that at this level they should be aware of the necessary punctuation. Then focus on useful lexis such as *trek* and the compound noun *foothills*.

Answers

1 Leaving/Having left at 6 am, 2 Not wanting to waste time,
3 leading to the foothills of the Central Range
4 Reaching/Having reached 5 Covered in snow, they
6 Descending/Having descended to a river,
7 built centuries ago 8 feeling hungry, 9 Realising that would mean more snow, 10 Having decided to carry on,
11 Looking back at that moment, 12 bearing in mind

5 If necessary, give the students an example of an eventful journey of your own, including participle clauses. Explain that they may write in the first or third person, perhaps using the text in Exercise 4 as a model. Give them about ten minutes to do this in class, then check their work for accuracy. Alternatively, they can write their account for homework. In both cases, choose some students to read their accounts to the rest of the class.

See the Workbook and CD-ROM for further practice.

Reading and Use of English

Prefixes

1 Point out that Part 3 often tests prefixes, and that some of the words in the exercise could appear in the exam. Give pairs a couple of minutes to do this, then go through the answers. If time allows, ask the class which other prefix mistakes they have heard.

Answers

1 inconveniently 2 decreased 3 ensure 4 imprecise
5 incapable 6 inevitably 7 non-existent 8 unrealistic

2 Point out that the words they form are all C1 level. Elicit the answers quickly and move on to Exercise 3, which focuses on the meanings of these prefixes.

Answers

1 under 2 re 3 over 4 mis 5 bi 6 out 7 anti 8 inter

3 Ask the class whether they have similar prefixes (or prefixes with similar meanings) in their first language(s), then give groups a few minutes to do both tasks. Point out that most of these prefixes can be used with different parts of speech. Elicit some of the answers, giving the rest of the class time to note down the correct words formed. Elicit suggestions for the prefixes not used in the exercise too.

Answers

a) re b) anti c) inter d) out e) under f) over
g) bi h) mis

Suggested answers

redo, reinstall; antivirus, anticlimax; interchange, interpersonal; outperform, outsmart; underweight, underachieve; overcook, overweight; bilateral, bicentennial; misinform, misunderstanding

Prefixes not used in Exercise 2: dis – giving a word the opposite meaning (disinterested, disagreeable) il – not or no (illegal, illiterate) mono – single or one (monosyllabic, monolingual) post – after or later than (postgraduate, postwar)

See the Workbook and CD-ROM for further practice.

Part 3

4 Give the class no more than a minute to do this gist-reading task and then elicit the answer.

Answers

to go (midnight/cross-country) skiing

5 Pairs study the example for a minute or two. Elicit the answers, and suggest they ask themselves similar questions for each item. Tell the class to do the exam task on their own, and allow no more than ten minutes for this as they have already spent time gist reading and studying the example. Point out that in the exam, suffixes are often more common than prefixes, but in this exercise there are five prefixes and one compound noun. Read through the Exam tip with the class. When they have finished, elicit the answers together with the affixes and compound, focusing on the fact that some words require both a prefix and a suffix (see Unit 8).

> **Answers**
>
> **1** adjective, add -ed or -t   **2** positive   **3** un-

Exam task

> **Answers**
>
> **1** background   **2** incomparable   **3** luxurious   **4** unexpectedly   **5** unbroken   **6** inexperienced   **7** uninterrupted   **8** intention

Listening

Part 2

1 You may want to explain that this festival dates from the time of the Inca civilisation prior to the arrival of Europeans in the 16th century. The Inca religion saw the sun as the most important factor in daily life, bringing light and warmth – hence the festival each June 24.

Let students use their dictionaries, if necessary, for these mainly C1-level nouns. You may want to elicit some verb forms such as *applaud*, *celebrate*, *participate* or *rehearse*.

> **Suggested answers**
>
> **1** Both photos show how the people of Cuzco celebrate the festival. The first shows a man looking very serious sitting in a special chair. I think he is being carried by a group of men – I can just see their heads. He's dressed in a colourful way and he could represent the Sun God. I think this must be part of an important ceremony. The other photo shows women in traditional costume leading a pretend animal through the streets. I think it's supposed to be a llama. I think this could be part of a procession from the church and we can see crowds of people watching.
> **2** Events like this can unite communities and provide identity, especially to peoples whose culture may have been affected by colonisation.
> **3** They are enjoying themselves, probably because of the occasion, the chance to meet extended family and friends, good food, dressing up, getting a day off from hard work in the fields or factories.

2 Give pairs two or three minutes to do this, possibly prompting by giving the key words to the first question (see below) as an example. Go through the answers, pointing out that although the answers here are all nouns – and that is generally the most common part of speech for answers in Part 2 – in other tests that may not be the case.

> **Answers**
>
> **1** words, city, because, buildings: noun phrase   **2** Cuzco, designed, shape: noun (phrase)   **3** Incas, houses, without, cold: noun   **4** problem, some, not, her: noun   **5** rehearsals, impressive: noun   **6** surprised, wide range, parade: plural noun   **7** builders, first made, stones: plural noun   **8** read, no, ancient Festival: plural noun

3 [1.05] Refer the class to the Exam tip then tell them to work on their own. Play the recording through twice, without pausing. Give everyone a minute to check they have answered all the questions and that their spelling is correct, then go through the answers.

If you wish, photocopy the recording script on page 71 for the students and ask them to underline the sections which give the answers.

Exam task

> **Answers**
>
> **1** (an) open-air museum   **2** a mountain lion   **3** windows   **4** (fierce) sun   **5** folk dancing   **6** (multi–coloured) costumes   **7** models   **8** spectators

> **Recording script**
>
> *You will hear a research student called Ava O'Neill talking about visiting Cuzco in Peru. For questions 1–8, complete the sentences with a word or short phrase. You now have 45 seconds to look at Part Two.*
>
> The Peruvian city of Cuzco is a total experience, from its location 11,000 feet up in the Andes mountains, its history as the ancient capital of the Inca Empire and its unique culture, to (1) <u>the blend of Inca and Spanish architecture from different centuries that has led to researchers referring to it as an open-air museum</u>.
>
> Its origins actually go back over a thousand years, but it was in the 13th century that the invading Incas reached Cuzco. They (2) <u>planned and built the city so that it resembled a mountain lion</u>, and districts and individual streets still bear the names of body parts such as the head and back, while the tail was formed by straightening the point where two rivers joined.
>
> Although night-time temperatures in Cuzco can be quite mild, that is certainly not the case all year round. (3) <u>On account of that, many of the original Inca homes there lacked windows</u> and had just a single door, which would have been covered by a thick mat during the chillier months. There would also have been a straw roof that had to be replaced every few years.
>
> My colleagues and I were there in late June, and I noticed on the first afternoon that (4) <u>a number of the others were looking distinctly uncomfortable as the fierce sun began to beat down, but as an Australian I'm accustomed to that</u>. The height above sea level was another matter, leaving all of us short of breath at times, especially when climbing the steep hills around the city.
>
> Having arrived a couple of days ahead of the Festival of the Sun, we were able to watch some of the performers practising for the big day. (5) <u>What really stood out for me was the folk dancing</u>, though some of the concerts and parades were well worth watching, too.

On the 24th, the day of the Festival itself, the city centre was packed as the procession set off. (6) The multi-coloured costumes were fabulous, even more varied than I'd imagined, as the participants moved slowly up the hill to the ancient site called Saksaywaman where the main ceremony would take place.

That is where the magnificent walls are located. Standing nearly six metres tall and measuring up to 400 metres in length, they were built of huge stones that fitted together perfectly. Given that some of them weighed 200 tons each, the only way the Incas could have achieved that, my research indicates, is by (7) sculpting models in lighter materials to the exact size and shape required, and then reproducing them in stone.

I stood there marvelling at the sight of the walls, and at the colourful scene as the ceremony began. Looking at the vast crowds of (8) spectators, I recalled a paper written by a local historian which made the point that in Inca times there weren't any. In one way or another, all the thousands of people at the Festival in those days were participants.

4 If you wish, give students an example of a festival you have been to. Try and use a variety of structures and vocabulary in your example to encourage them. Let them work in pairs and talk about the festivals they choose. Monitor as they are speaking and go over any problem areas at the end of the exercise. If time, choose a few students to tell the class about their chosen festival.

| See the Workbook for further practice. |

Speaking

Making comparisons

1 Use this exercise as a review of comparisons. Tell pairs or individuals to make the necessary changes in each sentence, which involve comparison of both adjectives and adverbs. Focus particularly on modifying expressions such as *a bit*, *not quite* and *nowhere near*. Point out that these structures could be tested in Reading and Use of English Parts 3 and 4 (see key word transformations on page 28 in Unit 3). Check students' work for accuracy and then elicit more examples of each structure, including those in the first sentence of each question. You may also want to discuss some of the cultural issues, e.g. April Fool's Day, raised here.

Answers

1 any less tea than they did in the past.   2 a lot more frequently there.   3 quite so / as many public holidays as some other countries.   4 far / much / a lot less common than it used to be.
5 nearly so / as likely to marry young as years ago.   6 near so / as widely celebrated internationally (as it is now).   7 isn't half as much fun as April Fool's Day.

2 Tell pairs to think about which customs have changed in recent times, and what makes their country different from others. Monitor for accuracy. You may want to get them to write down some of their sentences, and read them out to the class – especially if they are particularly interesting or amusing – but take care in a multilingual class that nobody offends other nationalities.

Part 2

3 🔘 *1.06* Refer the class to the Quick steps, then to the instructions. Remind them that in the exam there will be six photos for both candidates to have a long turn each. Make sure they understand how the task works by asking questions such as 'How long do you speak for?' and 'When does the other candidate speak?' Point out that Luisa and Emilia are both strong Advanced students, and play the recording once without pausing. Play it again if necessary, then elicit the answers. Refer students to page 108 of the Speaking guide.

Answers

1 1 and 2   2 Yes   3 She says the children's parents probably gave them more thought.

Recording script

Teacher: Luisa, it's your turn first. Here are your pictures. They show people with presents in different situations. Compare **two** of the pictures, and say what significance the presents might have for the people, and how those people might they be feeling.

Luisa: OK erm, in this picture there's quite a lot of people at what looks like a wedding. Or maybe it's after the ceremony itself, because of, er, the way the couple are dressed, and there's a lot of presents for them on the table, still wrapped in paper. In this one, on the other hand, there is a child opening a present at a party and looking very happy. It could be a toy that she's asked her parents for, or perhaps she just like surprises, because the present seems a lot more important to her than to the couple, who at the moment are probably thinking about other things, like their future together – starting with their honeymoon! The little girl is obviously feeling much more excited than the couple about the present, but they're enjoying the occasion and later they will have time to see the gifts their relatives and friends have given them. Perhaps nice things for their new home, and that will make them happy, too.

Teacher: Emilia, who do you think has given the most thought to their choice of present?

Emilia: Well, it's likely the people at the wedding chose something from a list they were given of possible presents, so they probably thought a bit less about what to buy than the parents of the little girl. Unless of course she told them what to get! Um, I think that would be quite unusual for a girl of that age.

---

4 🔘 *1.06* Play the recording again, pausing if necessary until the class have clearly identified the target structures, then elicit the answers. Also highlight the fact that both students try to avoid repeating the language of the questions, and use their own words instead.

Answers

the present seems <u>a lot more</u> important to her <u>than</u> to the couple
The little girl is obviously feeling <u>much more</u> excited <u>than</u> the couple
they probably thought <u>a bit less</u> about what to buy <u>than</u> the parents

5 You may want to put the class into different pairs to accustom them to working – as is likely in the Speaking exam – with partners they may not know. Tell the As to talk for no more than one minute (Bs could time them) before the Bs briefly answer their question.

Monitor pairs, ensuring that the Bs do not interrupt the As until the minute is up. Read the Exam tip with them. When they have all finished, tell them to change over and repeat, making different comparisons.

Ask them to assess their performances.
Tell pairs to be honest in their self-assessment and constructive in their comments about their partner's performance. Elicit some self-assessment comments only, and ask about any particular difficulties they may have had, such as keeping going for the required length of time – or limiting their speaking to one minute.

Writing

Part 2: report

1 Tell the class these are all expressions they may find useful when writing reports, as well as other text types such as reviews. They should know the twelve words given, but you may want to point out that *aims* and *outlines* are verbs here. Give pairs a couple of minutes to fill in the gaps, taking any vocabulary questions – there are some useful topic-related expressions such as *book ahead*, *impose regulations*, *overall reaction*, *further research*, *facilities for the disabled* and *admission fees*. Check their answers and go straight on to Exercise 2.

Answers

1 sum 2 recommendation 3 solution 4 purpose
5 balance 6 outlines 7 recommend 8 short
9 consider 10 course 11 aims 12 recommending

2 Give pairs two or three minutes to do this, ensuring they have a written list of complete expressions they can refer to later when writing their own reports. Point out that reports tend to be written in quite a formal style: the more formal expressions would be quite acceptable in written reports but less common in spoken language, except possibly in formal speeches.

Go through the answers. With a strong class, elicit more in each category, e.g. *this report is intended to show; it might be advisable to; in conclusion.*

Answers

Introduction: The purpose of this report is to; This report outlines; This report aims to
Recommendations and suggestions: My recommendation is; One possible solution would be to; I strongly recommend that; should consider; The best course of action would be; I have no hesitation in recommending
Conclusion: To sum up; On balance; In short
Quite formal: The purpose of this report is to; I strongly recommend that; The best course of action would be; I have no hesitation in recommending

3 Elicit the situations quickly, then get pairs to discuss improvements. Allow time for them to write their sentences, then check. Do a round-up with the class of their ideas, though remind them that some of these expressions are rather formal for everyday spoken language.

Suggested answers

1 The owners should consider refurbishing it.; I strongly recommend having it repainted.
2 One possible solution would be to provide free overnight accommodation. I have no hesitation in recommending an enquiry into how this occurred.
3 My recommendation is that more covered areas are provided. The best course of action would be to postpone the festival until the rain stops.

4 Let the class study the exam task for about 30 seconds, then elicit the answers. Suggest they ask themselves questions like these whenever they first look at a Part 2 report task. You could refer them to the Writing guide on page 103, which they could study for homework.

Answers

1 a popular festival in your country 2 Your tutor has asked you to write it for other students. 3 a description of the event, including where and when it takes place; how popular it is and why; changes you think should be made

5 Allow a minute or two for everyone to gist read the text, label the paragraphs and note down yes/no answers to the two questions. Check and then move on.

Answers

Paragraph 1 – C
Paragraph 2 – D
Paragraph 3 – A
Paragraph 4 – B
1 Yes 2 Yes

6 Allow plenty of time for pairs to go through the text, then elicit the answers.

> **Answers**
>
> **1** a) The aim of this report is to   b) rather fewer … than, a little more generous   c) In conclusion,   d) consequently, I would recommend + noun + infinitive without *to*; I would also suggest they consider + *-ing*
> **2** held each December; Attracting over 200,000 visitors annually
> **3** (Suggested answers) sweet festival, picturesque town, chocolate as art, the world's greatest, most impressive, fascinating, something to appeal to all, delights, opportunities to learn, make a real difference, of particular interest, informative, hugely enjoyable, leaves a pleasant taste in the mouth, delicious

7 Allow half a minute for this, then elicit the answers. Ensure that everyone understands the task.

> **Answers**
>
> **1** an interesting, lesser-known sight in your country
> **2** your manager; the agency you work for wants to promote more a lesser-known tourist sight in your country.
> **3** a description of the sight, its significance to your country, how it could become better-known internationally

8 Give groups a few minutes for this brainstorming activity, but don't elicit answers.

9 Tell the class it doesn't matter if they choose the same topic as the others in their group. Get them to work on their own, first noting down points to include and then putting those under the headings they choose. If they don't use headings, suggest they just put 'para 1' etc. to organise points. Allow about five minutes for this, then move on to Exercise 10.

10 Allow 35–40 minutes only for students to write their texts, as they have already studied the task and planned their report. Remind them to leave a few minutes at the end for checking.

Model answer

The caves near the coast

Introduction
This report looks at the magnificent Nerja caves in southern Spain. Located in the foothills of the impressive Almijara mountain range, the caves were discovered completely by chance about 50 years ago when a group of boys were out exploring.

Ready for visitors
Since then further parts of the cave system have been opened, steps cut into the rock and lighting installed in order that visitors can see the spectacular geological features there. These include vast caverns and what is said to be the world's biggest limestone column.

Part of Spain's history and culture
In Spain the caves are now officially listed as a historic site. There is a section, currently closed to the public, containing wall paintings that are many thousands of years old, and these have immense historical significance. In addition, one of the caverns is so big that it is used for the Festival of Music and Dance, featuring famous Spanish opera singers, classical musicians and dancers.

Conclusion
In short, the Nerja caves are one of this country's greatest attractions, and it is a pity that so few of the millions of tourists who come to the Spanish coast ever visit them. The best course of action, I believe, would be to advertise the caves more widely in other countries, and I would also recommend launching a publicity campaign in tourist areas. In the summer months, this could inform people that even when the temperature is 40 degrees, the air inside the caves is always cool and fresh.

> See the Workbook and CD-ROM for further practice.

3 Behaving and interacting

Unit objectives

TOPICS	human behaviour & relationships
GRAMMAR	review of reported speech
VOCABULARY	collocations; idioms with *keep*
READING AND	Part 4: key word transformations;
USE OF ENGLISH	Part 5: multiple-choice questions
WRITING	Part 2 letter: formal / informal / neutral style; layout
LISTENING	Part 1: short texts, multiple-choice questions
SPEAKING	Part 3: suggesting, (dis)agreeing, asking for opinions

Listening

Collocations

1 Allow pairs to use dictionaries for some of the expressions here, and be ready to take questions. Point out that more than one of the odd-words-out will go into certain groups. When they have finished, quickly elicit the meanings and move on to Exercise 2, which practises many of them.

> **Answers**
>
> **1** brief (relationship) **2** family (friend) **3** personal (friend)
> **4** absent (parents) **5** strong (relationship) **6** mutual (friend)

2 Point out that this activity is similar in format to Speaking Part 2. Give pairs a couple of minutes to do this, encouraging them to use the expressions from Exercise 1. You may want to elicit or provide more collocates for *relationship*, e.g. *happy*, *difficult*, *serious*, *poor*, *intense*.

> See the CD-ROM for further practice.

Part 1

3 Make sure the class are familiar with the format of Listening Part 1, i.e. that they will hear each extract twice consecutively and have to answer two questions about it while they listen.

Go through the answers. Suggest they ask themselves these questions whenever they do Listening Part 1, but point out that they will sometimes have to use their intuition (both here and in the exam), for instance the situation is likely in extract 1, implied in extract 2, and stated in extract 3.

With a very good class, ask them to state what the focus of each question is also. This will help them think about the language to listen out for, e.g. 1 – reason; 2 – function of giving advice; 3 – the topic; 4 – function of expressing surprise; 5 – shared opinion; 6 – attitude.

> **Answers**
>
> Extract 1 – 1 conversation, probably at home 2 Jack and Emily, a couple 3 a problem Jack has at work
> Extract 2 – 1 a conversation at home 2 two people 3 a TV news story
> Extract 3 – 1 a conversation in a café 2 two students 3 flat sharing

4 🔊 *1.07* Refer the class to the Quick steps and the Exam tip, then play the Part 1 recording through without pausing. Allow 30 seconds for the class to make sure they have answered every question, then go through the answers.

If you wish, photocopy the recording script on page 72 for the students and ask them to underline the sections which give the answers.

Exam task

> **Answers**
>
> **1** B **2** C **3** A **4** C **5** C **6** B

> **Recording script**
>
> You will hear three different extracts. For questions 1–6, choose the answer (A, B or C) which fits best according to what you hear. There are two questions for each extract.
>
> **Extract one**
>
> *You hear a couple, Jack and Emily, discussing a problem he has at work.*
>
> *Now look at questions one and two.*
>
> F: So what happened? I thought you two got on well?
>
> M: We used to, yes. But when he heard last week that <u>the new contract had been assigned to me, he suddenly stopped speaking</u>, and today he started a row when he saw me in the canteen. At one point it got so heated he threatened to take it up with the general manager, though I knew he wouldn't actually go that far. Any more than he'd walk out on the job, as at one point he said he might.
>
> F: I suppose in a way you can understand why he's so upset. He's been there longer than you, after all. But I know he can be quite aggressive, so rather than try to discuss it rationally with him I think <u>I'd do my utmost to keep out of his way until he calms down a little</u>. I'd certainly find somewhere else to eat, or a different time. When does he usually have lunch?
>
> M: Twelve-thirty.
>
> F: So how about having lunch at noon, for the time being at least?
>
> M: That makes sense, yes.
>
> **Extract two**
>
> *You hear two people discussing a news story that they have just watched on TV.*
>
> *Now look at questions three and four.*

M: That was quite interesting, wasn't it? <u>Particularly the bit about eye contact. So, looking straight at you says nothing at all about whether someone's telling you the truth or not.</u>

F: Yes, I've always thought that was a myth. It's not as if cleverer liars were unaware some people believe that, and I'm sure some criminals try it on. Though, as the reporter said, the police aren't fooled, they just ignore it.

M: But the effective ways of spotting liars – I liked some of those used by detectives, such as noticing how quickly people answer a question.

F: Yes, it's logical they'll take longer to reply if they're having to invent a complicated story. <u>And also getting suspects to give their version of events in reverse order. It'd never occurred to me before,</u> but that must be much harder if you're making it up as you go along.

M: And what did you think of the figure quoted for the number of lies the average person admits to telling each day? About one and a half, wasn't it?

F: Yeah, though I suspect some of them might have been lying about how often they lie!

Extract three

You hear two students, Amelia and Ollie, in a café talking about flat sharing.

Now look at questions five and six.

M: So after all the flat sharing we've done over the last couple of years, what lessons do you think we've learned?

F: The crucial thing is the initial choice of people. Because if you don't take your time doing that, you can end up with all kinds of tensions. What you really want is a relaxed relationship with the others, and also the hope – especially if you're new in town – <u>that they'll take you out to places and help you socialise.</u>

M: I suppose you might get lucky and hit it off with the first ones you meet, and if they happen to be sociable types, <u>you'll get to hang out with their mates, too</u> – but more often it's about making compromises with acquaintances, isn't it?

F: It's certainly true you have to compromise when it comes to keeping the place clean. I think I have pretty high standards of hygiene and I wouldn't share with anyone – male or female – who was really messy, but I don't think there's any need to make a fuss about trivial things. <u>I mean, it's a real pain if some perfectionist starts complaining just because, say, you leave the odd mug in the sink.</u>

> See the Workbook and CD-ROM for further practice.

Grammar

Reported speech

1 Go over the example with the class. Explain that they do not need the reporting verbs in the direct speech version, but they can add fillers such as 'So' or 'Oh' to make their sentences sound more natural if they wish. Give them a few minutes for them to underline the changes and write their answers, then go on to Exercise 2 without checking the answers first.

2 🔘 *1.08* Play the recording twice if students need longer to make any corrections, pointing out that *wasn't able to*

is also possible for 4. Give pairs plenty of time to note the changes, then go through these. Point out that in 8, *'d* is a contracted form of *would*, and that no change is needed to *there* owing to the context, or elicit these points from the class. Also ask for examples of other common differences between direct and reported speech such as *here → there*, *tomorrow → the next day*.

Answers

1 Are you still living in the same flat?   **2** No, I'm not. I moved out last week.   **3** Why did you leave?   **4** I couldn't study properly.   **5** What was the problem?   **6** A few months ago, my flatmate started learning the violin.   **7** Have you found a quieter place now?   **8** Yes I have, and I think I'll enjoy living there.

Words that change

1 no 'whether', he → you, was → are
2 no 'that', he → I, wasn't → 'm not, He → I, 'd moved → moved, the previous week → last week
3 'did' added, he → you, 'd left → leave
4 he → I, hadn't been able to → couldn't
5 word order: verb 'be' before subject, had been → was
6 earlier → ago, his → my, had started → started
7 no 'whether', 'have' added, he → you, 'd found → (have) found, by then → now
8 'yes' added, he → I, had → have, no 'that', he → I, thought → think, he → I, 'd → 'll

---

Recording script

F: Are you still living in the same flat?

M: No, I'm not. I moved out last week.

F: Why did you leave?

M: I couldn't study properly.

F: What was the problem?

M: A few months ago my flatmate started learning the violin.

F: Have you found a quieter place now?

M: Yes I have, and I think I'll enjoy living there.

---

3 In this exercise, the class should focus particularly on the highlighted reporting verbs and the grammar connected with them. Give pairs two or three minutes to do this, referring if necessary to the Grammar reference, page 90. Go through the answers, eliciting more examples with each reporting verb.

Answers

1 Some students suggested going / suggested we (should) go sightseeing on Monday.
2 Your brochure said that I would get a room in a high-class hotel.
3 correct
4 correct
5 He threatened his daughter that he would not speak to her / not to speak to his daughter again if she married that man.
6 The radio told us not to go anywhere because of the snow.
7 The electric company apologised for not telling / having told me the lights would go out.
8 Socrates never promised that his students would actually learn anything specific.

4 Tell students to do these individually, then check their work for accuracy. Allow any correct variations.

> **Suggested answers**
>
> **1** S/he denied (that) s/he had broken / S/he denied breaking my coffee mug.   **2** S/he asked (me) if s/he could help me.
> **3** S/he suggested sharing/(that) we (should) share that flat together.   **4** S/he apologised for waking/having woken me up.
> **5** S/he promised (that) s/he would pay me back / S/he promised to pay me back at the end of the/that month.
> **6** S/he warned me not to touch/against touching that wire while the electricity was on.
> **7** S/he threatened to/that s/he would call the police if s/he didn't get out immediately.   **8** S/he said the next day was Saturday. S/he told us not to wake her before noon.

5 Explain that they must use reporting structures after each verb, but it doesn't matter whether the sentences are true or not. Go over the example as a class. Point out that they sometimes need to use different words to show what was actually said, e.g. *I was late so I explained* becomes *I'm afraid*. Let students have a few minutes to do these on their own, then check their work in pairs. When everyone has finished, elicit a couple of answers to each.

> **Suggested answers**
>
> **1** to get up in the morning. 'I'm not getting up in the morning!'   **2** me to her party. 'Do you want to come to my party?'   **3** that I'd been using her make-up. 'You've been using my make-up, haven't you?'   **4** me not to forget to call. 'Don't forget to call!'
> **5** me to drink lots of fluids. 'You should drink lots of fluids.'
> **6** not telling me the truth. 'I'm afraid I didn't tell you the truth.'
> **7** to drive me to the station. 'Shall I drive you to the station?'
> **8** I get one like that. 'You should get a phone like this!'

> See the Workbook and CD-ROM for further practice.

Reading and Use of English

Part 5

1 This activity introduces the topic of the Reading text, which raises the issue of whether we now prefer to text, email, tweet and so on rather than actually talk to people. Give pairs a couple of minutes to discuss, then ask the class what they think.

2 Give students, working on their own, about two minutes to answer this gist question. Point out they will need to read the whole text to answer it. Elicit very brief answers and don't go into any detail at this stage.

> **Answer**
>
> No, it isn't.

3 Explain that the wrong answers are 'distractors' designed to tempt candidates into giving the incorrect answer, and tell pairs to highlight the parts of the text that relate to each option. Allow pairs five minutes to do this before going through the answers, focusing on the relevant parts of the text. Then get them to do the exam task on their own, allowing about fifteen minutes for this. Go through the

answers and take any vocabulary questions. If time allows, ask the class to respond to the ideas in the text: *Is electronic communication different from human contact? What about video conferencing? Will conversation survive? If so, why?*

> **Answers**
>
> **1** the first paragraph   **2** 'People strolled in the street outside likewise, with arms at right angles, necks bent and heads in awkward postures.'   **3** A: 'every one, whatever their age group', so not mainly young people   B: 'The scene resembled something from an old science-fiction film.' It only resembled a film; it was in fact real.   D: 'The place was oddly quiet' 'Odd' means strange, and there is no suggestion he found the silence pleasant.

Exam task

Read through the Exam tip and Quick steps with the class before they begin.

> **Answers**
>
> **1** C   **2** B   **3** B   **4** B   **5** A   **6** C

> See the Workbook and CD-ROM for further practice.

Reading and Use of English

Idioms with *keep*

1 Point out that the first six of these idioms are C1 level according to English Profile, and all of them are used quite often in conversation and writing (the other two are C2 level). Give pairs a couple of minutes to work out the answers, then check. Ask if they have similar idioms in their own language(s). If there is time, elicit or present some more idioms, e.g. *keep your head above water, keep someone on their toes.* You could also let students work in pairs to tell their partners the last time: a) they found it hard to keep their cool, b) they found it difficult to keep their word, c) they kept their fingers crossed, d) they couldn't keep a straight face. The partner should ask questions to elicit as much information as possible.

> **Answers**
>
> **1** do what they said they would   **2** stay calm   **3** watch for someone to appear   **4** try not to be noticed   **5** continue to know   **6** let them know what's happening   **7** stop yourself smiling or laughing   **8** hope things will turn out well

Part 4

2 Allow pairs a few minutes to go through the instructions and analyse the example item using the three questions here. Make sure everyone knows how to do this task type: if in doubt, ask concept questions such as 'What is the *word given* in the example?' Read through the Quick steps, answer any other queries that may arise and then go through the questions with the class.

> **Answers**
>
> **1** It has become the adjective *constant*. A noun or noun phrase.   **2** It becomes a noun. Plural.   **3** Keep a low profile. Positive.

3 Read through the Exam tip. Give students, working on their own, about 12 minutes to write their answers. They should find the clues helpful, but remind them that they will not have these in the exam. Point out that forms tested here have all been practised in this Unit. When everyone has finished and checked their work, go through the answers.

Exam task

> **Answers**
>
> **1** have sprung up | recently / recently | sprung up   **2** she would resign | unless they increased   **3** me (from) / my | keeping track of   **4** promise / promising | to keep / stay in touch
> **5** apologised for not keeping / apologised for breaking | its / their   **6** him | to stand up to

Speaking

Asking for opinions, suggesting, and (dis)agreeing

1 Give pairs a few minutes to do both parts of the task, then check. Elicit other ways of expressing the same functions, e.g. *What do you think about this one?; It might be an idea to move on now; I entirely agree; I'm not convinced about that.*

> **Answers**
>
> **1** just   **2** leave   **3** point   **4** feel   **5** move   **6** along
> **7** thoughts   **8** inclined
> a 4, 7   b 2, 5   c 1, 6   d 3, 8

Part 3

2 Give pairs a minute to look at the task, then elicit the answer. Then go through the Quick steps.

> **Answers**
>
> Success in life, good health, appreciation of natural and artistic beauty, coping with problems, good relationships with relatives and friends – as possible factors in human happiness.

3 🔘 *1.09* Play the recording once through without pausing, then ask the class for the answers.

> **Answers**
>
> **1** Yes   **2** Yes   **3** No

Recording script

Teacher: Here are some things that can help make people's lives happy and a question for you to discuss. First you have some time to look at the task. Now, talk to each other about how important these factors might be in making individuals happy with their lives.

Leona: Shall I start?

Mia: Yes, go ahead.

Leona: OK then, the first thing is I don't think you have to be particularly successful in your studies or work to be happy, but if you aren't doing as well as perhaps you should, then that can make you quite unhappy.

Mia: I'd go along with you there. I mean, people who get top marks in everything don't seem any happier than the rest of us, and those who do badly don't look miserable all the time, either. So maybe 'success' isn't the right word, and it's actually 'knowing you've done your best' that brings happiness.

Leona: Right. So how do you feel about this one, a healthy lifestyle?

Mia: Oh, I think that's really important. If you do plenty of exercise and keep fit, you feel a whole lot better all the time. Definitely.

Leona: I'm not so sure about that. Footballers don't always look that happy with life, do they? And there are plenty of people who do no exercise but still seem very contented.

Mia: But only if they stay healthy, surely? People who often get sick are unlikely to enjoy life very much.

Leona: That's true. So maybe it's best to do just enough exercise to reduce the risk of illness.

Mia: OK, shall we move on to the next one?

Leona: Uh-huh.

Mia: What are your thoughts on this?

Leona: Appreciating the beauty of nature.... yes, that can make a real difference.

Mia: Yes, but if we're talking about life in general, what about people who live in cities and don't often get to see the countryside? Can't they be happy?

Leona: Well yes, because even in the biggest cities there are parks where you can see trees and flowers, and birds.

Mia: And how about art?

Leona: That depends, really. Some people get pleasure from it but others don't.

Mia: It can make a big difference if you can lift your spirits whenever you want to by just looking at beautiful pictures, or listening to music.

Leona: That brings us on to the next one, doesn't it? And I think that's essential, because if you let things get you down you can never truly be happy.

Mia: Oh, I totally agree. Worrying or getting angry all the time must make you very unhappy. You've got to be able to deal with your problems or life becomes a nightmare.

Leona: And that's so much easier if you have support from family and friends, like it says in the last point.

Mia: Absolutely. It's often lonely people who look sad, the ones who live by themselves and don't have any friends.

Teacher: Now you have about a minute to decide which factor has the most positive effect on human happiness.

Leona: Well, I think we more or less agree that whether you're successful or not doesn't make that much difference, that staying healthy matters but without going to extremes…

Mia: And that appreciating natural and artistic beauty can certainly help…

Leona:	Yes, but for me it's being able to handle everything that life throws at you that makes all the difference to overall happiness. Friends and relatives can help, but in the end it's down to you as an individual.
Mia:	Hmm, my own view is that humans are social beings, and that means we can't ever be genuinely happy unless we have a close relationship with others.
Leona:	Well, I don't think we're going to entirely agree on that last point.
Mia:	No; let's leave it at that.
Teacher:	Thank you.

4 🔘 *1.09* Play the recording once or twice more, pausing if necessary if some students are having difficulty keeping up as they make notes. Go through the answers, suggesting they use some of these expressions when they do the task.

> **Answers**
> 1 Shall I start?, Yes, go ahead.
> 2 I'd go along with you there, How do you feel about this one? What are your feelings on this?
> 3 Right (c)   I'm not so sure about that (d)
> But…surely? (d)   That's true. (c)
> Yes, but … what about …? (d)   Can't…? (b)
> And how about…? (d)   Oh, I totally agree. (c)   Absolutely. (c)   My own view is that (d)
> 4 I don't think we're going to entirely agree on that last point.; No; let's leave it at that.

5 Read through the Exam tip with the class. Then time the activity so it lasts no longer than three minutes in total (you may want to indicate when the first two minutes are up).

6 When pairs have finished, ask them if they covered all the points, and whether they reached agreement. Ask which they chose as the most important, with brief reasons. You may want to tell the class that these points are based on Carl Jung's '5 Basic Factors for Happiness'. Ask the class if they can suggest more factors, such as 'helping others'. Remind students to refer to page 109 of the Speaking guide for further help.

Writing

Register

1 Give students two minutes to read through the texts and establish the style of writing. Elicit where they would use the different styles, e.g. formal in a job application, informal to a friend or relative, neutral to somebody they don't know well or don't know socially, e.g. a teacher. Then ask them to read the texts again to find the different points. They can do this in pairs. By doing this they should come to understand which kinds of words are usually used in each style, e.g. phrasal verbs are commonly used in informal and neutral writing but not in formal writing.

> **Answers**
> 1 A informal, B neutral, C formal
> 2 phrasal verbs – A: get back to, find out, get together; B: meet up
> long/less common words – C: apologies, extremely, occupied, position, fortunately, announced, convenient
> exclamation marks – A: I've got the whole of next week off!
> passive verb forms – C: has been announced
> impersonal expressions – C: it has been announced
> conversational expressions – A: Sorry, had a lot on, what with, stuff like that, we're in luck, the whole, tell you what, if that's OK with you
> abbreviations – A: pm, asap
> very short sentences – A: Sorry not to get back to you sooner.
> contracted forms – A: I've, we're, I've, I've, let's, that's B: don't
> formal linking expressions – C: on account of, in addition to, however, therefore

2 Point out that these register mistakes all occurred in informal texts, and that the grammar is correct. Give pairs two or three minutes to do these, then check.

> **Suggested answers**
> 1 persons → people (sign in a lift)   2 regret → 'm sorry (letter to an employee)   3 execute → carry out (business document)
> 4 awaken → wake up (children's story)   5 thus → so (scientific paper)   6 consume → eat, have (research document)

> See the Workbook for further practice.

Part 2: letter

3 Remind the class that they should always use the input task in Writing as a guide to the register they need to use in their own text. Give pairs two or three minutes to underline or note down the informal features of the extract, and then analyse the content for what they have to do. Explain that letter tasks often involve expressing a number of functions, as in this task. Go through the answers with the class. Refer students to page 101 of the Writing guide.

Answers

1 Informal/neutral – certainly not very informal. Conversational *so* to begin a sentence; dash; contracted form *I've*; informal expressions *got, lots of, all sorts, tips*; ending the last sentence with a preposition, rather than using a formal preposition + *which* relative clause. But no slang, abbreviations or exclamation marks; there is the use of the long-ish words *behaving* and *experience*, and the paragraph is written in complete sentences.

2 a) ask for advice: 4th sentence **b)** describe events: 1st sentence **c)** report a conversation: 2nd sentence **d)** give reasons: 3rd sentence

4 Give pairs a minute or so to do this, then check.

Answers

a) 5th paragraph **b)** 1st paragraph **c)** 3rd paragraph **d)** 1st paragraph **e)** last line **f)** 2nd paragraph **g)** 1st paragraph **h)** 4th paragraph

5 Not all students may know these conventions, or the layout, so check their answers. Advise against beginnings such as *Dear friend*. Elicit alternatives, with contexts, e.g. *love* only for relatives, partners or very close friends.

Answers

Dear + first name of recipient; *Best wishes* + first name of sender (probably the most often used for friends/colleagues). *Hi* + first name, *Hello* + first name, Hi; All the best, Best, Bye for now, Cheers, Love, Lots of love, Kisses etc. (all followed by first name). All on separate lines.

6 Give pairs plenty of time to do the three parts. Tell them whether you want them to underline the relevant parts of the text or not.

Answers

1 Ashley (never *Dear friend*)
2 a) Use of first name after *Dear*; informal words e.g. *thanks, great*; punctuation: use of dashes, exclamation marks; contracted forms; short sentences, e.g. I got the impression he's a bit down; phrasal verbs, e.g. *get back to, move in*; informal linkers, e.g. *and, so*; shortened forms, e.g., *sorry, hope to*; informal ending *Best wishes* plus first name only
b) Longer, more complex sentences, e.g. *Ever since…*, *He clearly didn't want…*; longer words, e.g. *unfortunately, impression*; addition links, e.g. *firstly, finally*
3 He <u>admitted</u> he'd done almost no housework
<u>said</u> he was sorry
<u>explained</u> he'd been suffering from a long-term injury
he <u>promised</u> he'd make more of an effort
4 a) far from it **b)** to cap it all **c)** all hours **d)** have a word with **e)** as yet **f)** had little effect **g)** left out

7 Pairs study the task for a minute. Give them time to read the Quick steps as well. Elicit answers and remind them to ask themselves questions like these whenever they do an email or letter writing task.

Answers

1 Your penfriend will have to make his/her own friends as he/she will not be with you. **2** informal/neutral **3** language level, shyness, best ways of making friends in your country with reasons

8 Tell students to work in pairs, making notes for each prompt. Ask if they can think of other good ways of meeting people, e.g. doing voluntary work.

9 Point out that this is just one suggested way of organising the text for this task. Some students may prefer to cover the points about language learning and shyness in one paragraph, they may want to use fewer paragraphs in total, and so on. Look at some of their plans before they begin writing their letters.

10 Allow 35–40 minutes for students to write their letters, as they have already studied the task and planned their text. Remind them to leave a few minutes at the end for checking. This could be done for homework. Tell them not to forget about the Exam tip – it's very important that they always use their own words.

Model answer

Dear Thomas,

Thanks for your letter. I'm glad to hear all's well, and that you're looking forward to your stay here. It'll be hot, so bring plenty of factor 50 sunscreen!

But please don't worry about your Italian. You certainly speak it well enough to chat with people, and I'm sure you'll become even more fluent after you've been here a couple of weeks. It doesn't matter if you make a few grammar mistakes – that's all part of learning, isn't it?

You'll find that people here are really friendly. They love talking and it's easy to get into conversation wherever you are. In fact, it's the best place in the world to get over any shyness!

That means you can make new friends in places like cafés, and even on the bus or train. Like anywhere, though, it's easier if you have a common interest, so perhaps you could join a club in the town where you're staying. For instance, I know you're crazy about mountain biking, just as many young Italian people are – so why not find a local cycling club on the Internet and contact them?

Also, you could check out the online ads for language exchanges: you spend half the time talking in your language and half in the other person's language. Of course, lots of people here want to learn English, and you want to practise your Italian – so it'd be ideal. It's also a fantastic way of getting to know people!

Write back when you can.

All the best,

Alessandro

> See the Workbook for further practice.

4 Selling and spending

Unit objectives

TOPICS	money & business
GRAMMAR	review of passive forms; causatives
VOCABULARY	fixed phrases; phrasal verbs with *out*; money vocabulary
READING AND USE OF ENGLISH	Part 2: open cloze; Part 7: gapped text
WRITING	Part 1 essay: addition links, achieving balance
LISTENING	Part 3: long text, multiple-choice questions
SPEAKING	Part 4: expressing & justifying opinions

Reading and Use of English

Part 7

1 Ask the class the first question, if necessary giving prompts such as job security/risk taking, fixed income/variable income, having a boss/being one's own boss, acting on others' decisions/decision-making. For the second question, point out that they could discuss running not-for-profit organisations such as charities, town councils, etc.

2 Refer the class to the first Quick step, then tell students to do the exercise on their own before comparing notes with their partners. Make sure everyone understands *recession*. Go through the answers and, if there is time, ask the class to give reasons for their answers.

> **Answers**
> 1 C
> 2 Suggested answers: narrative of events, with thoughts on each; by matching paragraphs with the sequence of events and the writer's response to them.

3 Focus attention on the Quick steps and the Exam tip, then give the class 12–15 minutes to do this, working on their own. When they have finished, remind them to check they have answered all the questions, then go through the answers.

> **Answers**
> 1 E   2 C   3 A   4 F   5 B   6 G; D not needed.

4 Tell pairs they can use their dictionaries to check these business terms, with reference to the contexts within the paragraphs. Go through them with the class when they have finished.

> **Answers**
> market trends: the direction and movement of demand for a product
> promotional activity: using publicity and/or advertising to raise a product's profile
> raising finance: obtain loans
> marketing and pricing: promoting and selling products, deciding the price of an item for sale
> points of sale: places where items are available for purchase
> launching products: introduce a new item on the market
> focus groups: people brought together to discuss a particular subject
> market research: gathering information about consumers' needs and preferences
> target audience: group of people to which an advertisement or product is directed
> the paying public: people who actually buy the products

Phrasal verbs with *out*

5 Give students working on their own a few minutes to note down their answers. Go through these with the class, eliciting more example sentences with each. Ask them about the use of *splash out on* in the text: is it meant to be ironic?

> **Answers**
> get out: go to different places and meet people
> start out: begin to do something in life or business
> sell out: there are no more of that to buy
> try out: use something to see if it works
> splash out on: spend a lot of money on (*splash out on* contrasts with 'second-hand', so its use is probably ironic)
> check out: examine to be certain it is true or suitable

6 Give pairs two or three minutes to do these. Be ready to take any questions on topic related vocabulary such as *currency* and *foreign exchange*, and point out that the last two items require passive forms of phrasal verbs. Check answers and elicit more examples with some or all of the phrasal verbs.

> **Answers**
> 1 chill out   2 ran out   3 check out   4 got out
> 5 backed out   6 cutting out   7 kicked out   8 bailed out

> See the CD-ROM for further practice.

Grammar

Passive forms

1 Refer students to the Grammar reference on page 91 if you feel they may have difficulty with some of the more complex structures. Point out that phrasal verbs have passive forms (questions 2 and 3), and then get pairs to work on the answers together. Go through the answers, eliciting more examples of each use.

Answers

1 email confirming your purchase is sent to you. – c
2 office was broken into last night. – b (and possibly d)
3 was held up by a gang dressed as clowns. – d
4 is reported to have made a loss. – f
5 must always be followed. – a
6 is thought that unemployment will rise. – e

2   Encourage the use of a range of passive structures for the first part of the text, but not the impersonal *It …* form, as this will be practised in the second part. Be ready to feed in vocabulary as they do the activity. Ask for examples of each of 1–6 when everyone has finished.

Suggested answers

1 The card is placed in the machine, then the PIN number is entered, the OK button is pressed, the money is sent to the seller's account, the purchase is completed.
2 Items are added to the shopping basket, the total bill is calculated, payment is made by credit or debit card, the purchase is completed, the goods are sent.
3 A SIM card with credit is bought, the cost of each call/text is deducted, more credit is added to the account.
4 An item is chosen from a list, a bid is made, the item is won, the payment is made online, the item is sent to the winner's address.

Sentences with *It*

Suggested answers

2 It is thought that more than 50% of households now use online shopping.
3 It's claimed that pay-as-you-go mobile phones are cheaper to use.
4 It has been estimated that twenty million people have bought items on eBay.

Causatives: *have/get/want something done*

3   Tell pairs they must use a form of the structures in the heading. When they have corrected the sentences and done the matching, check their answers. Elicit more examples of each type using different verb tenses, and ask what the difference is between *get* and *have* in these structures (*get* is more informal, and not possible for use in c).

Answers

1 c – to have not your bicycle stolen → not to have your bicycle stolen
2 a – we don't want the money be wasted → we don't want the money (to be) wasted
3 b – you get it to be repaired → you get it repaired.

4   Pairs take turns asking and answering these. Go through the answers when they have finished, asking for a number of possibilities for questions 3 and 4.

Suggested answers

1 Yes, I must get / have it repaired.   2 I want it cut short, please.   3 I told them I'd had a lot of items stolen.
4 I would have / get all my meals made for me by a top chef.

5   Tell the class, working on their own, to follow the same instructions as for Reading and Use of English Part 4. Also point out that three of these require causative forms, and three passives. Check their written answers for accuracy.

Answers

1 had my old printer fixed by   2 it had not / hadn't been held up   3 want a smart new suit made
4 is believed to have been caused
5 had his bank account closed because
6 was reliably reported yesterday

See the CD-ROM for further practice.

Reading and Use of English

Fixed phrases

1   Explain that these useful expressions are the kind of phrases that may be tested in Reading and Use of English Part 2. Give pairs a few minutes to do these, then go through the answers. Elicit more examples with some or all of them.

Answers

1 in order to do something   2 except   3 much less   4 In the first place   5 in general   6 more than anything else
7 forever   8 for now but not permanently

2   Encourage students, working individually, to use their imagination when completing these. When they have finished, elicit a couple of answers for each.

Suggested answers

1 selling it.   2 get a new car.   3 tourism.
4 I'll have to make do with this old one.   5 an Australian.
6 everyone is now online.   7 I get a well-paid job.
8 I want to see the world.

Part 2

3   Give the class a minute or two to gist read the text, then ask them the answer.

Suggested answers

1 Thinking that it would never happen, or become popular.
2 Those that make people's lives easier and also conserve energy.

4   Give the class, working on their own, ten minutes to do the exam task using the clues. You may also want to point out that one of the items (6) tests a passive form that they have practised. After they finish, go through the answers, also eliciting the words that form fixed phrases.

Exam task

> ### Answers
>
> **1** about **2** which **3** From **4** of **5** large **6** are **7** both
> **8** may / might / could
> Fixed phrases: **1** all about **4** a (long) history of **5** by and
> large **8** may / might / could well

Listening

Money vocabulary

1 Tell pairs to use the context to work out the meanings in each case, then elicit the answers.

> ### Answers
>
> **1** neither makes money nor loses money; spend more than it earns
> **2** having lots of money / wealthy; too expensive for people to buy
> **3** having taken more money out than was in the account; money charged by a bank for borrowing
> **4** financially successful; cannot pay debts so unable to continue in business
> **5** having a lot of money; have just enough money for essentials
> **6** total before tax; made to pay tax
> **7** spending less money than usual; unfairly expensive (informal)
> **8** money to pay for something; provide financial protection

See the CD-ROM for further practice.

Part 3

2 Point out that these questions focus on the topic of the listening to follow. Pairs discuss these points based either on their own experiences or what others from their own country tend to do when they go to other cities or countries to study. Elicit some of their answers, correcting any mistakes made with the target language.

3 🔘 *1.10* Read through the Quick steps and the Exam tip. Play the recording without pausing, then check the answers. Also ask which key words the class underlined. If you wish, photocopy the recording script on page 73 for the students and ask them to underline the sections which give the answers.

> ### Suggested underlined words
>
> **2** believes, most useful, discounts **3** theft, laptop, wished
> **4** surprised, how much, spending **5** debt, felt **6** advice, in debt

> ### Exam task
>
> **1** B **2** D **3** A **4** B **5** A **6** C

Recording script

You'll hear an interview with a student called Liam, who talks about the financial difficulties he faced during his first year at university. For questions 1–6, choose the answers (A, B, C or D) which fits best according to what you hear.
You now have 70 seconds to look at Part 3.

Interviewer: My guest today is Liam Callaghan, a second-year history undergraduate who had some difficulties managing money when he went to university. So Liam, as a student suddenly living on your own in another city, I suppose the first thing you had to do was set up a bank account. How did you decide which bank to choose?

Liam: I'd already arranged a student loan and to be honest my only concern was getting my hands on the cash as easily as possible. All the main banks had branches on campus which meant any of them would do. And I wasn't bothered about things like how much they'd let you borrow on a credit card, or whether they'd let you overdraw without having to pay interest. So (1) <u>it came down to what they were giving away in an attempt to attract people like me. In the end, I opted for the one offering the clock radio</u> in the hope it would get me up in the mornings, though it wasn't very successful in that respect.

Int: And how did you get on managing your finances? Did you find having a student card made things much cheaper?

Liam: Yes and no. Things like cut-price tickets to see films are fine if that's what you like doing, but I'd rather stay at home with a take-away meal on my lap as I (2) <u>watch DVDs. Now they *are* something you can make quite a saving on, with some websites giving a percentage off if you're in full-time education. The same goes for textbooks and other stuff you need.</u> I also saved a lot on long-distance coach fares, much more than going by train. People talk about how a student railcard can save you money, but the fact is you get a better deal by booking your tickets in advance, like everyone else.

Int: Did you go home during the holidays, or stay in the hall of residence?

Liam: I went home at Easter, though unfortunately while I was away my room was broken into, and my laptop stolen.

Int: Really?

Liam: Yes, (3) <u>I shouldn't have left valuables there, I realise that now.</u> Especially as they weren't insured. I'd assumed they'd be covered by my parents' policy because I'd got them to extend their contents insurance to cover my things while I was away, but when I tried to claim I was told it only applied during term time. The laptop was the biggest loss, both financially and in terms of losing all the study notes I had on it, not that they'd be any use to anyone else even if they could access the files. A friend asked me why it was so easy for them to get into my room, but the truth is there's not much you can do to keep determined thieves out when almost everybody's away.

Int: That must have been a shock for you. Did you have to replace the laptop yourself?

Liam:	Yes, and it was at that point I noticed I was spending too much overall. It wasn't that I was splashing out on suits or shoes or anything like that, or going to expensive nightclubs and restaurants. Actually, if my friends and I did go out, we'd usually just have a coffee somewhere and share a cab home, which actually worked out cheaper than taking the bus. (4) <u>No, what was taking me over budget was paying back some cash I'd borrowed a few months earlier. I'd got it from one of those money shops without working out the true interest rate.</u>
Int:	So now you owed money. How did you feel about that?
Liam:	Well, in situations like that it's always easy to say somebody should've warned you, but really I had no-one else to blame but myself. I also knew that my family weren't in a financial position to come to my rescue so (5) <u>it was up to me to sort it out. I didn't doubt my ability to do so</u> as long as the people I owed money to kept their side of the agreement, and I had no reason to believe they wouldn't. It all worked out in the end, but it wasn't an experience I'd care to repeat.
Int:	What would you advise other students in that situation to do?
Liam:	Firstly, to face up to reality. There's no way the debt will go away and there's no chance of talking lenders into charging you less interest on it, so all you can do is (6) <u>find out the minimum amount they'll accept over how many months, make a deal on that basis and stick to it.</u> There's always a temptation to relieve the pressure by borrowing elsewhere and paying that back over a longer period, but all you're doing then is prolonging the situation. Of course, to reduce any debt you've got to cut back on your spending, though I wouldn't recommend going without essentials. Yes, you have to economise – but don't forget to eat.
Int:	Liam Callaghan, many thanks.

> See the Workbook and CD-ROM for further practice.

Speaking

Expressing opinions

1 Give pairs a couple of minutes to do as many of these as they can, then elicit the answers from the class. Explain that they will need these expressions particularly in Speaking Part 4. Ask if they know any other expressions, e.g. *In my opinion, I'd say that.*

> **Suggested answers**
>
> **1** opinion, view, feeling **2** point **3** seems, appears **4** see, understand **5** honest, frank **6** 'm concerned, know, can tell **7** believe, think **8** my

Part 4

2 🔘 *1.11* Tell the class they will hear expressions from Exercise 1, and that they should use these as cues for the speakers expressing the opinions they have to identify here. Play the recording through without pausing, then check the answers.

> **Answers**
>
> **1** E **2** S **3** S **4** B **5** B **6** S

Recording script

Teacher:	For young people, what are the advantages and disadvantages of being financially independent from their parents?
Esra:	The way I see it is that achieving financial independence is an essential step in becoming an adult. <u>For one thing</u> it enables you to set up your own home and run your own life, and I think that makes you act more responsibly when you realise just how difficult it can be to make ends meet. Though that, of course, can also be a big disadvantage if you're not good at limiting your spending, <u>because</u> then you might end up not being able to pay your bills. And that can lead to all sorts of problems.
Teacher:	Do you agree?
Stefan:	In part, yes. But it seems to me that being independent has a different meaning for people from different backgrounds. <u>The point is</u>, if your family are poor they can't support you if things go wrong and you can end up living on the street, whereas richer people know their parents will always, er, bail them out. <u>So</u> that's a big advantage if you're well off.
Teacher:	How can we reduce the huge difference in wealth between rich and poor countries?
Stefan:	To my mind, the obvious solution is for richer countries to increase the amount of aid they give, which at present is only a tiny fraction of their national income. And not just make promises for the future. They must actually do it: now, and every year.
Esra:	My own view on this is that aid alone isn't enough, however much is given. <u>It's clear that</u> too much of it disappears into the pockets of corrupt officials. It's far better in the long-term to increase investment and trade so that poorer countries can develop their own industries. Where aid is necessary, for instance to improve children's health, it's best done by specialist international charities like Oxfam rather than by governments.
Stefan:	Both are important, in my opinion.
Esra:	Yes I agree, but I think we need to consider how we can make state aid more effective before we start talking about increasing it.
Teacher:	Some people say 'Money can't buy you happiness'. How far do you agree with this?
Esra:	Oh definitely! <u>I mean</u>, you only have to look at all those miserable rich people in the glossy magazines and on TV to see that. There are much better ways of becoming happy than getting rich, like having lots of good friends, doing a worthwhile job, having interesting hobbies and so on.
Teacher:	What do you think?
Stefan:	Yes, it's true. <u>In fact</u>, the actual process of getting rich probably makes those people unhappy because they're too busy trying to make money to enjoy life. Though again I'd say there's a difference here between rich and poor, <u>because</u> having very little money is without doubt a cause of great unhappiness for some people. For them a bit more money might actually bring a little happiness.
Teacher:	Thank you.

3 🔘 *1.11* Play the recording again, pausing where necessary. Then elicit the answers, and any others the class may know, e.g. *everyone knows that, all the evidence shows.*

> **Answers**
>
> for one thing   because   the point is   so   it's clear that   I mean   in fact   because

4 Explain that in this activity they will play the roles of 'examiners' and 'candidates'. Tell the candidates that they can ask for repetition of the questions, but the examiners cannot rephrase or add to the printed questions apart from adding the prompts given in the bullet points. You may want all groups to begin simultaneously so that you can ensure that each 'Part 4' lasts about five minutes. 'Candidates' should have their books closed. Stress the need for 'the examiners' to be polite and constructive in their comments. Read through the Exam tip with the class.

Do a class round-up when all groups have finished, asking what difficulties the 'candidates' encountered, e.g. *keeping talking for that length of time*, and make a note of these for future classwork.

Students can read page 111 of the Speaking guide for homework.

Writing

Addition links

1 Pairs should be able to do this fairly quickly. Point out that these expressions are normally followed by a comma. Check their answers.

> **Answers**
>
> *For the initial point*: firstly, for a start, in the first place, to begin with
> *For subsequent points*: additionally, as well as that, besides, furthermore, in addition, more importantly, moreover, on top of that, secondly, what is more, worse still
> *For the last point*: above all, finally, last but not least, lastly, most importantly
>
> Quite formal: furthermore, moreover, what is more
> Fairly informal: as well as that, on top of that
> (The remainder of the phrases for subsequent points are neutral.)

2 Students work on their own, ticking the relevant boxes. Tell them they can choose any of the ads, and write three or four full sentences about it using any of the prompts. Encourage the use of passive forms, e.g. *The reader is told ...* . Elicit answers for both ads when they have finished, and check their written work.

Part 1: essay

3 Let pairs study the exam instructions, notes and comments, then go through the answers.

> **Answers**
>
> **1** the impact of advertising on society; for your tutor.
> **2** Any two of: our everyday lives, what we buy, the economy
> **3** One or more of the three handwritten comments, in your own words.

4 Give pairs plenty of time to read the extracts and discuss the answers. Be ready to help out with any new vocabulary such as *intrusion*, but encourage them to try to work out the meanings from context first. Go through the answers with the class.

> **Answers**
>
> **1** a) B   b) A   c) C
> **2** A: some television adverts might make us smile; B: a few can make you laugh out loud
> **3** a) A: to begin with, then, worse still; B: firstly, in addition, above all; C: furthermore, moreover
>   b) A: although; B: even if; C: on the other hand
>   c) A: We are surrounded, you are met; B: it has been said; C: is seen by some

5 Give pairs about five minutes to study the text and note down answers to the questions. Be ready to take any vocabulary questions if they are unable to work out the meanings for themselves.

> **Answers**
>
> **1** To define the term 'advertising', state the purpose of the essay, and tell the reader which two main points it will deal with.
> **2** what we buy (2nd paragraph), the economy (3rd paragraph)
> **3** "It makes people spend money on things they don't really need": consumers are being sold unnecessary items. "A lot of people work in advertising companies": Advertising is a major industry. Besides employing thousands of people itself,...
> **4** The economy. It creates employment both directly and indirectly. Its influence on what people choose may have been exaggerated; nowadays more objective sources of information about products are available online.
> **5** Addition links: firstly, in addition, secondly, besides, what is more, also
>   Contrast links: but, however, though, conversely
> **6** consumers are being sold; the cost is passed on; could otherwise be employed
> **7** Last paragraph; 'My own view is ...'.

6 Give students, working in pairs, about five minutes to do this brainstorming activity, making notes as they do so. Encourage them also to come up with relevant points of their own.

7 Remind students about the point in the Exam tip. Allow no more than 35 minutes for the actual writing, as they are already familiar with the task and have made notes for their essay. Then give them five minutes for checking, referring to page 15, possibly in pairs. Remind students to look at page 99 in the Writing guide.

Model answer

Advertising is all around us. At home, while travelling and at work, we are urged to buy this or do that via every conceivable form of media. The effects of this are felt by consumers and non-consumers alike.

Advertising is seen by some as one of modern society's evils. It makes us greedy, they say, targeting even young children with its consumerist message. Furthermore, it constantly interrupts our television programmes, blocks up our email inboxes and wastes our time with unsolicited phone calls. On the other hand, some advertisements are visually beautiful, others make you think and a few can make you laugh out loud. Moreover, some are truly memorable: almost everyone can recall their favourite TV ad from childhood.

How effective is advertising? Even if an advertisement fails to motivate consumers to buy the product immediately, the positive feelings it creates may make them do so months or years later. In addition, individuals often tell friends about ads they like, potentially influencing their choices, too. Some consumers, however, are put off products by ads they find annoying or offensive. Furthermore, new media advertising is less successful than old. Television commercials rely on engaging a largely passive audience, whereas internet users tend to be too busy to click on ads.

Overall, therefore, advertising in the digital age is declining as a factor determining what people buy, especially given the range of items available online from all over the world. It remains, though, a powerful influence on our lives, not least because so many adverts are so cleverly made.

See the Workbook for further practice.

5 Health and sport

Unit objectives

TOPICS	health & sport
GRAMMAR	conditionals including mixed forms & forms without *if*
VOCABULARY	word building; suffixes; compound adjectives
READING AND USE OF ENGLISH	Part 3: word formation; Part 8: multiple matching
WRITING	Part 2 proposal: purpose links, text organisation
LISTENING	Part 2: sentence completion
SPEAKING	Part 2: commenting on partner's pictures

Listening

Word building

1 Tell groups they can use dictionaries if necessary, but remind them to be careful with the spelling of words like *surgical* and *preventative* when they note them down. Go through the answers, eliciting meanings and usage where this may not be clear, e.g. *clinical*. Ask them for the negative of *conscious* (unconscious) and words formed from it.

> **Answers**
>
> | Verb | Noun | Adjective | Adverb |
> |---|---|---|---|
> | X | medicine / medic | medical | medically |
> | X | surgery / surgeon | surgical | surgically |
> | prevent | prevention | preventative | X |
> | treat | treatment | X | X |
> | prescribe | prescription | X | X |
> | infect | infection | infectious | infectiously |
> | X | consciousness | conscious | consciously |
> | X | clinic / clinician | clinical | clinically |

2 Tell students to stay in their groups and use expressions from Exercise 1 to talk about the photos. Be ready to feed in other vocabulary such as *operate*, *anaesthetic*, *vaccinate* and *diagnose*, and elicit words formed from them.

Part 2

3 Let pairs work on this for a minute or two, but tell students they should do this on their own in future, whenever they do Listening Part 2. Go quickly through the answers, without taking any questions on the items themselves. Refer students to the Quick steps.

> **Answers**
>
> types of people: 1, 6   a school subject: 3   places: 8
> a physical object: 7   abstract ideas: 2, 4, 5

4 🔘 1.12 Refer the class to the Exam tip then play the recording through, without pausing. Allow a minute at the end for them to check they have answered all the questions and that their spelling is correct, then go through the answers. If you wish, photocopy the script on page 74 for your students and ask them to underline the sections which give the answers.

Exam task

> **Answers**
>
> **1** classmate   **2** academic ability   **3** math(s) / mathematics
> **4** job satisfaction   **5** medical knowledge   **6** (current) students
> **7** acceptance letter   **8** (the) developing countries

> **Recording script**
>
> *You will hear a woman called Lin Cheng talking about becoming a medical student. For questions 1–8, complete the sentences with a word or short phrase.*
>
> *You now have 45 seconds to look at Part 2.*
>
> When you tell people you're studying to be a doctor, they sometimes ask whether your family first suggested it to you, but although my parents are delighted that I'm now a medical student, I don't think they ever mentioned it back then. (1) <u>The only one who did, I think, was a classmate</u> who I'd given first aid to after she'd got hurt in the gym. I think the gym teacher was quite impressed and she too may have felt that I might become a doctor, but if so she kept it to herself.
>
> Actually none of the other staff ever suggested it to me as a possible career, either. On reflection, (2) <u>they probably considered I lacked the academic ability necessary to do a degree in medicine</u>. I think I can prove them wrong about that, though it's certainly one of the longest and most demanding degree courses.
>
> But that wasn't what I first did at university. I'd always liked science subjects and when I was seventeen I had to make my mind up which courses I wanted to apply for. For a while (3) <u>I was considering doing I.T. but in the end I had to face up to the fact that maths wasn't one of my strong points;</u> unlike chemistry, which I'd always been reasonably good at, and that's what I decided to do.
>
> I enjoyed my time at university and in the main found the course interesting, but I knew I wasn't suited to doing chemical research and after graduation I started work as a research assistant at the local medical centre. There I came into contact with doctors for the first time, and listening to them (4) <u>it soon became apparent to me that the job satisfaction they feel is of a kind experienced in no other profession</u>. Other careers may offer the high salary, the respect of other people or the lifelong opportunity to keep learning, but not that.
>
> I then did some work experience at a local nursing home, which gave me a real insight into the world of health care. Helping the patients there was immensely rewarding and (5) <u>I wished I could have done more for them, though of course my medical knowledge at that time was far too limited for me to do so.</u>

Motivated by this experience I did some studying in my spare time, and six months later I felt ready to take the admissions test required by medical schools. I also attended open days at several of them. I'd assumed that I would learn most from the staff there, and although talking to them was certainly worthwhile, (6) it was what current students had to say that really made an impression on me, and helped me make my mind up which place would suit me best.

Eventually I sent off my application form, stating my choice of school. I heard nothing for quite some time and I was half expecting a rejection, but then I received a message – an email I think it was – asking me to go for an interview. And then, finally, (7) that unforgettable moment when the acceptance letter popped through the door. I immediately texted all my friends, inviting them to a celebration party.

I'm about halfway through my course now, well aware that I still have an enormous amount to learn before I can even begin to think of myself as a doctor, but I do have some tentative ideas for the future. I want to spend the first few years in a local hospital, perhaps working in A & E, and maybe then do a PhD at a specialist hospital. But (8) ultimately what I'd most like to do is apply my medical knowledge and skills to helping those where the need is greatest: the developing countries. One of the great attractions of medicine as a career is that it offers enormous flexibility, and opportunities to make a difference to the lives of some of the most vulnerable people on Earth.

See the Workbook and CD-ROM for further practice.

Grammar

Conditional forms

1 Point out that this exercise practises basic conditional forms, mixed conditionals and conditionals without *if*. Give pairs plenty of time to read the relevant parts of the Grammar reference on page 93, match the endings and decide why the other answer is wrong. When you go through the answers, explain that all the options given in 1–6 are possible conditional forms, with the exception of *in case* in 4C – which the Corpus shows is a common error at this level. Elicit some examples of this form used correctly. Also ask which forms are quite formal: *had* in 5, *should* and *were* in 6.

Answers

1 not D – incorrect conditional form, should be *would feel* or *would have felt*
2 not B – incorrect conditional form, should be past perfect: *had not been*
3 not D – *supposing* means *what if* (C uses double *will* for polite requests)
4 not C – *in case* does not mean *if*; it should be *if, as long as* etc.
5 not A – *provided (that)* is not used in the past/third conditional
6 not B – *providing, as long as*, etc. are not normally used for negative ideas

2 Point out that in some of these sentences more than one answer is possible. Give pairs a couple of minutes to do these, then check. You could then get them to do the exercise again, this time using *if*.

Answers

1 under the condition → on condition   2 unless → provided/on condition (that), as/so long as   3 prove → proved
4 the users had → the users would have had
5 am → would be
6 in case → provided (in case that → as long as)

3 Tell the class that these transformations practise structures that could be tested in Reading and Use of English Part 4. Allow five minutes for them to write their answers, working on their own, then check their answers for accuracy.

Answers

1 be feeling ill if he hadn't / had not eaten too much.
2 your temperature goes down, I'll / I will call the nurse.
3 weren't / were not a caring person, she wouldn't / would not have become a doctor.
4 (that) you do plenty of exercise, you will lose weight.
5 Had Mr Kay known he was unwell, he would / might / may not have carried on working.
6 surgery is not required, patients are usually treated in one day.
7 Eva has to go into hospital; what will her children do?
8 you need a further appointment, please inform the receptionist.
9 that you have a prescription, you can buy medication on this website.
10 there to be any accidents, paramedics will treat minor injuries.

4 Tell pairs to use as many of the conditional forms they have practised as possible. When they have finished, ask volunteers for some of their ideas.

Suggested answers

1 I wouldn't have become so infatuated with that boy band if I'd known they'd be history a year later.
2 I'd still be living in the countryside if my parents hadn't decided to move to the city.
3 I would take the job as long as it paid a good salary.

See the Workbook and CD-ROM for further practice.

Reading and Use of English

Part 8

1 The questions could be discussed in pairs or small groups. Allow a couple of minutes for them to complete the table, then go through the answers. Ask where other sports, e.g. squash or cycling might fit in this table (14 and 3.5 injuries per 1,000 hours respectively).

Answers

1 rugby   2 basketball   3 running   4 Alpine skiing   5 tennis

2 Highlight the pronunciation of words such as *tear*, *ache* and *bruise* (and point out they can be either verb or noun) before they begin. Allow the use of dictionaries for parts of the body, and/or be ready to feed in lexis such as *muscles* or *ligaments*.

> **Suggested answers**
>
> dislocated shoulder, fractured toes, sprained ankle, torn muscle, twisted knee, aches in their calves or thighs, blisters on their feet, bruises on their legs, soreness on their heels, swelling of their ankles

3 Encourage brief answers only, as this is the topic of the exam reading text.

4 Give the class 30 seconds to do this, then elicit the answers. Remind them always to look quickly at these features whenever they do Part 8.

> **Answers**
>
> An article in five parts; experienced athletes/runners giving advice on how to avoid injuries.

5 Give pairs a minute or two to do the underlining. Or, if you prefer they do not write in the book, ask them to note down the key words. Go quickly through these when they finish, without spending too much time on individual words as opinions will vary. Leave discussion of the ideas in the text until after they have done the exam task.

> **Suggested answers**
>
> 2 no evidence, other sports, avoid 3 building, muscle, prevent 4 stretching, prior, no beneficial 5 beginning, programme, don't, too much 6 surface, little difference, risk 7 avoid, speeding, end 8 advisable, exercise, after, finish 9 biggest risk, not, breaks 10 pain, not, must, stop

6 Focus attention on the Quick steps and Exam tip, then give the class, working on their own, 12–15 minutes to do the exam task. Go through the answers, and if time allows elicit the relevant phrases and sentences in the text. You may also want to focus on some of the distractors, e.g. Question 1 / the first sentence of E. You can then discuss the ideas in the text.

> **Answers**
>
> 1 D 2 C 3 A 4 C 5 D 6 A 7 E 8 B 9 D 10 B

7 Tell pairs to use the context to work out the meanings of these useful expressions. Go through the answers, eliciting examples of some or all of them in other contexts.

> **Answers**
>
> a) needless to say b) take issue c) make a point of doing d) strike a balance between e) the key to f) conventional wisdom g) no … whatsoever h) the odds are against i) step by step j) take note of k) on the grounds that

> See the Workbook and CD-ROM for further practice.

Reading and Use of English

Suffixes

1 Explain that these are the kind of words often tested in Reading and Use of English Part 3, with the kinds of changes (noun to verb, adjective to adverb, etc.) that are frequently required. Give pairs plenty of time to do these,

using their dictionaries if necessary. Remind them to be very careful with spelling.

> **Answers**
>
> competence: 1 noun 2 -ence 3 competent 4 drops final 't' 5 adjective
> inevitably: 1 adverb 2 -ly 3 inevitable 4 drops final 'e' 5 adjective
> leadership: 1 noun 2 -ship 3 leader 4 no 5 noun
> participant: 1 noun 2 -ant 3 participate 4 drops 'ate' 5 verb
> pointless: 1 adjective 2 -less 3 point 4 no 5 noun
> qualification: 1 noun 2 –ion/-ation 3 qualify 4 'y' changes to 'i', 'c' added 5 verb
> skilful: 1 adjective 2 -ful 3 skill 4 drops final 'l' 5 noun
> specific: 1 adjective 2 -ic 3 specify 4 drops final 'y' 5 verb
> statistical: 1 adjective 2 -al 3 statistic 4 no 5 noun
> summarise: 1 verb 2 -ise 3 summary 4 drops final 'y' 5 noun
> threaten: 1 verb 2 -en 3 threat 4 no 5 noun

Encourage pairs to think of further words with each of the suffixes. When they have finished, go quickly through these.

> **Suggested answers (all C1)**
>
> acceptable, changeable, renewable; existence, interference, reference; basically, formally, hourly; hardship, ownership, sponsorship; contestant, reluctant, tolerant; homeless, restless, speechless; accusation, clarification, complication; graceful, respectful, thoughtful; chaotic, idealistic, scenic; clinical, minimal, musical; authorise, generalise, recognise; deepen, strengthen, weaken

2 Explain that in some cases they will need to replace the suffix, but some (also) require a spelling change to the stem brought about by the addition of a suffix. Allow two minutes for this, then check.

> **Answers**
>
> 1 stressful 2 immensely 3 useless 4 inconvenience 5 apologetic 6 subsidise 7 cultural 8 happily

> See the Workbook and CD-ROM for further practice.

Part 3

3 Allow no more than a minute for this gist-reading the task, then elicit the answer.

> **Answers**
>
> Some athletes may not be able to afford it.

4 Pairs study the example for a minute. Check their answers.

> **Answers**
>
> noun to adjective; -(t)ial added

5 Read through the Exam tip with the class, stressing that all words given need to be changed. Give the class no more than ten minutes to complete the task as they have already spent time gist reading and studying the example. Remind them that in the exam, suffixes are often more common than prefixes, although sometimes (as in 8) both are possible. Elicit the answers, together with the changes in part of speech.

> **Answers**
>
> **1** noticeable (noun/verb to adjective)   **2** performance (verb to noun)   **3** technological (noun to adjective)
> **4** evolution (verb to noun)   **5** participants (verb to plural noun)
> **6** availability (adjective to noun)   **7** economic (noun to adjective)   **8** insignificant (verb to negative adjective)

Speaking

Compound adjectives

1 Give an example in context, such as *The school cross-country race takes place on Friday*. Pairs should be able to do these quickly, if necessary using dictionaries. Go through the answers, then elicit more compounds with one of the words in the compounds they formed, e.g. *cross-cultural, cross-border, cross-legged*.

> **Answers**
>
> fair-haired, first-rate, friendly-looking, full-length, high-risk, highly-qualified, left-handed, long-distance, record-breaking, twenty-kilometre, world-famous

> **Suggested answers**
>
> dark-haired, first-class, good-looking, full-time, high-speed, highly-paid, right-handed, middle-distance, record-setting, twenty-pound, internationally-famous

2 Tell the class only to use the compounds formed from the words in the boxes. Give pairs a minute or two to do this, then check their answers.

> **Answers**
>
> **1** fair-haired   **2** long-distance   **3** friendly-looking
> **4** full-length   **5** world-famous   **6** high-risk

3 Tell groups to try to come up with at least three compounds with each, using dictionaries if necessary. Go quickly through their answers, checking they understand the meaning and usage of each.

> **Suggested answers**
>
> hard-line, hard-hearted, hard-wearing, hard-up; open-air, open-ended, open-minded, open-mouthed; one-off, one-sided, one-stop, one-way; short-sighted, short-tempered, short-term, short-staffed

Now focus on compound adjectives with numbers and ask students to give example sentences. Then give groups three to five minutes to come up with different compound adjectives. Elicit two examples from each group.

> **Suggested answers**
>
> one-armed (bandit), one-night (stand), one-way (street); two-faced, two-piece, two-tone; three-piece (suite), three-star (hotel), three-point (turn); four-wheel (drive), four-fold (increase), four-stroke (engine)

See the CD-ROM for further practice.

Part 2

4 🔵 *1.13* Point out that Zeinab and Reza are both strong Advanced students, and play the recording once without pausing. Ask the class for their answers. If you wish, photocopy the recording script on page 75 for the students. Ask them to listen again and check their answers.

> **Answers**
>
> **1** The gymnast and the sailing crew   **2** Yes   **3** Yes

> **Recording script**
>
> **Teacher:** Zeinab, it's your turn first. Here are your pictures. They show people winning Olympic medals. Compare two of the pictures, and say how difficult it might have been for them to acquire the skills needed to reach this level, and how these people might be feeling.
>
> **Zeinab:** Well, they both show people competing in Olympic events. All three must have trained very hard to get to this standard because you have to be extremely fit either to be a gymnast or to sail this kind of boat. I'd say, though, that becoming a top gymnast takes a lot more practice in terms of balance and timing. On the other hand, the women in the boat have to learn to work closely together, to coordinate everything, so this isn't an individual sport like gymnastics. They're also racing against others at the same time, with the risk of collision, while the gymnast does his turn completely alone. That means, though, he's probably feeling very nervous right now, especially as the crowd and his opponents are all watching, waiting for him to make the slightest mistake. The sailors are possibly feeling less nervous than him, not least because there's nobody else around.
>
> **Teacher:** Reza, who do you think has put the most effort into acquiring their skills?
>
> **Reza:** Sorry, could you say that again, please?
>
> **Teacher:** Who do you think has put the most effort into acquiring their skills?
>
> **Reza:** My own feeling is that it's probably the relay runner. He's had to train as hard as a top sprinter in terms of fitness and becoming one of the fastest men in the world. He's also had to practise getting up to exactly the same speed as the incoming runner within the regulation distance, as well as the technique of taking the baton correctly and at just the right time. Because if he drops it, or impedes any of his opponents or breaks any of the other rules, his whole team will be disqualified.
>
> **Teacher:** Thank you.

5 `1.14` Tell the class that this time they will hear just the part that involves Reza. Play this once or twice, as necessary, then go through the answers.

> **Answers**
>
> **1** Sorry, could you say that again, please? **2** The relay runner **3** He had to train for speed and handover technique.

> **Recording script**
>
> Teacher: Reza, who do you think has put the most effort into acquiring their skills?
>
> Reza: Sorry, could you say that again, please?
>
> Teacher: Who do you think has put the most effort into acquiring their skills?
>
> Reza: My own feeling is that it's probably the relay runner He's had to train as hard as a top sprinter in terms of fitness and becoming one of the fastest men in the world. He's also had to practise getting up to exactly the same speed as the incoming runner within the regulation distance, as well as the technique of taking the baton correctly and at just the right time. Because if he drops it, or impedes any of his opponents or breaks any of the other rules, his whole team will be disqualified.
>
> Teacher: Thank you.

6 You may want to put the class into different pairs, A and B. Remind the A students to talk for no more than one minute before the B students answer their question in no more than half a minute. Monitor pairs, ensuring there is no interruption before time is up. When they have all finished, tell them to change over and repeat.

7 Refer students to the Exam tip. Remind pairs to be honest and constructive in their comments. Elicit some self-assessment comments only, and ask about any particular difficulties they may have had, particularly when commenting on their partner's pictures. Refer students to page 108 of the Speaking guide.

Writing

Purpose links

1 You may want to check they are clear which structures follow which links. Tell the class these are all links they may find useful when writing proposals, as well as when making suggestions other text types such as reports.

Then give individuals or pairs two minutes to choose their answers. Check these.

> **Answers**
>
> **1** to, in order to **2** so, so that **3** in order that, so that **4** in order to, so as to **5** so that I wouldn't, in order not to **6** So as to, To **7** so as not to, in order that you do not **8** in order to, so as to

2 Reassure the class that they don't need to go into a deep analysis of what motivates people to do these things; their own opinion or popular perception is enough. Elicit some

answers when pairs have finished, correcting any errors in usage of the links. If time allows, ask the rest of the class to suggest alternative purpose links in each case.

> **Suggested answers**
>
> astronomy – in order to study the stars and planets
> drawing – so as to develop a creative talent
> hiking – to spend time in the countryside
> martial arts – so they can learn how to defend themselves
> Pilates – to improve flexibility and strength
> pottery – in order to make useful or beautiful objects
> Salsa dancing – to have fun, in order to get fit, so they meet people
> scuba diving – in order to explore the sea under the surface
> vegetable gardening – so they can grow their own food
> Yoga – in order to learn how to relax, to develop a spiritual discipline

See the Workbook for further practice.

Part 2: proposal

3 Give the class 30 seconds to study the exam task, then go through the answers. Suggest they ask themselves questions like these whenever do a proposal task.

> **Answers**
>
> **1** a grant for new sports facilities **2** The Planning Director; to decide which sport should receive the money and how it should be spent **3** neutral or formal **4** which sport should be chosen, how the money should be spent, why spending it on your choice of sport would benefit people in the town

4 Refer the class to the Exam tip and tell them to gist read the text in no more than a minute, noting down their answers as they do so. Check these, and then move on.

> **Answers**
>
> **1** The missing sport (which sport should be chosen)
> **2** A sensible investment (how the money should be spent)
> **3** Improving people's lives (why spending it on your choice of sport would benefit people in the town)

5 Give pairs plenty of time to study the text, then check their answers.

> **Answers**
>
> **1** a) first paragraph: The aim of this proposal is to …; b) last paragraph: I would strongly recommend that … be …
> **2** Conditional. It is impolite to assume your proposal will be accepted, so it is better to use *would rather* than *will* to talk about the future: would be spent, would not be, would be, would be, would be, would be, would set up, would strongly recommend, would be
> **3** a) to (suggest), to (do this), so that (matches) b) Olympic-size, top-class, increasingly-popular, cost-effective c) as well as, moreover, also

6 Give the class 30 seconds to look at the exam task, then elicit the answers. Refer them to page 104 of the Writing guide.

7 Give groups three or four minutes to brainstorm ideas for each of their hobbies, but don't elicit answers.

8 Having read through the Quick steps, tell the class to work on their own, noting down points to include and then putting them under headings to write their plan. Allow four or five minutes for this.

9 Give students about 35 minutes for the actual writing, as they have already studied the task and planned their proposal. Remind them to leave time at the end for checking.

Model answer

Proposal for a new club

Introduction

The purpose of this proposal is to put forward a suggestion for a new hobby-based club for this college.

Fascinating and worthwhile

Reading is the ideal way to spend a quiet evening or a lazy weekend. It can cure boredom or stress by taking you into another world, cheaply and easily. Books can be bought, borrowed or – increasingly – accessed online. You can read them at home, while travelling or when on holiday, on a screen or on old-fashioned paper. They might be historical novels, biographies, science fiction, books of poetry or of any other genre; written in your first language or in the one you are learning. It is impossible to run out of books to read, even in a lifetime.

Sharing ideas

Discussing books with others makes reading even more enjoyable. By setting up a book club, meeting once a week in the library, the college would enable students to exchange opinions about books they have read, discuss issues raised by the content, and encourage each other to read more widely. Students could take turns suggesting a book of the week, which would motivate the others to finish it by the time they next met. If there is a film version of the book, the group could see that together, too.

Conclusion

Reading is an essential part of college life. I believe that a college book club would help make students more aware of the fact that it is also a highly pleasurable free-time activity.

See the Workbook for further practice.

6 Culture old and new

Unit objectives

TOPICS	the arts & entertainment
GRAMMAR	review of verbs + *-ing* or infinitive
VOCABULARY	collocations; frequently confused words
READING AND	Part 1: multiple-choice cloze;
USE OF ENGLISH	Part 5: multiple-choice questions
WRITING	Part 2 review: praising & criticising
LISTENING	Part 4: multiple matching
SPEAKING	Part 1: expressing likes, dislikes & preferences

Reading and Use of English

Collocations

1 The class should already know the adverbs, but may need to look up some of these mostly C1-level adjectives. Students can work in small groups. Give them a few minutes then go through the suggested answers. If there is time, elicit phrases or sentences with each, e.g. *a highly acclaimed new play.*

> **Suggested answers**
>
> eagerly / generally / widely anticipated
> absolutely / completely / perfectly / totally / utterly appalling
> highly distinctive
> highly / totally / wonderfully enjoyable
> absolutely / completely / totally / utterly hilarious
> deeply / highly / wonderfully imaginative
> dreadfully / highly / totally / utterly / generally overrated
> absolutely / completely / generally / totally / utterly pointless
> highly / wonderfully talented
> dreadfully / highly / utterly tedious
> highly / totally / utterly / wonderfully unconventional

2 Tell groups they can discuss the art forms themselves, the works or performances shown and/or the artists, performers or composers. Ask the class for some of their ideas when they have finished.

3 These questions focus on some of the points covered in the exam text. Students stay in their groups to do this quickly. Do not go through their answers at this stage as their own ideas will give them a reason for reading in Exercise 4.

> See the CD-ROM for further practice.

Part 5

4 Students working on their own should be able to do this gist-reading task in a couple of minutes. Quickly elicit some answers from the class and then move on. Explain that the title is a play on words. The original phrase would have been 'quick fix'(a quick fix is a fast solution but one that is usually only temporary).

5 Give pairs five minutes to do this. If you don't want them to write in the book, suggest they note down the paragraph number(s) for each question. When time is up, elicit the answers, without going into great detail about where exactly the part that deals with one question ends and another

begins. Remind the class this needs to be done quickly – there won't be time in the exam to spend long on this stage.

> **Answers**
>
> 1 paragraph 2 2 paragraphs 3–4 3 paragraphs 5–6
> 4 paragraph 6 5 paragraph 7 6 paragraph 8

6 Tell the class to work on the exam task individually, giving them about fifteen minutes for this. Go through the answers and take any vocabulary questions.

> **Answers**
>
> 1 D 2 A 3 C 4 B 5 B 6 C

> See the Workbook and CD-ROM for further practice.

Grammar

Verbs followed by the infinitive and/or *-ing*

1 Students work in pairs.They can refer to the Grammar reference on page 94 if necessary, but they should be able to answer these without doing so. Check both sets of answers. Then give them more time to add verbs to a–f (note that others like *a* are mainly modals) before eliciting some of these from the class.

> **Answers**
>
> 1 attempting – e 2 have – a 3 to go – b 4 listening / to listen – f 5 seeing – d 6 to join – c
> **b** arrange, appear, attempt, expect, manage, seem; e.g. *We arranged to meet at nine.*
> **c** assist, cause, encourage, forbid, order, teach; e.g. *My parents taught me to be polite.*
> **d** appreciate, can't help, fancy, miss, put off, resent; e.g. *They miss seeing each other.*
> **e** discover, find, hear, notice, see, watch; e.g. *I noticed a man standing there.*
> **f** begin, can't bear, commence, continue, hate, start; e.g. *He hates to get up / getting up early.*

2 Students do these individually, using their own ideas. Elicit a couple of answers for each.

> **Suggested answers**
>
> 1 playing every day. 2 to buy them. 3 people eat noisy food. 4 going in. 5 them to paint a beautiful landscape.
> 6 to be with the band. 7 them standing in the crowd.
> 8 you to go to the post-gig party.

3 Students will probably have studied these distinctions before, but it is clear from the corpus (CLC) that Advanced candidates often make mistakes with these forms. Give pairs plenty of time to do the matching and discuss the differences. Go through these carefully when everyone has finished, and elicit more examples with each form.

> **Answers**
>
> 1 a ii – intended; b i – involved, it was necessary
> 2 a i – attempted but it was impossible; b ii – did it as an experiment
> 3 a i – will always remember the experience; b ii – won't make the same mistake again.
> 4 a ii – did what I needed to do; b i – recalled the action
> 5 a i – am sorry about giving bad news; b ii – wish I hadn't said
> 6 a ii – refused to speak to them again; b i – paused while walking and spoke

4 Give pairs two or three minutes to find and correct the errors. Go through the answers, pointing out that *go on* in 7 is another verb that changes its meaning according to which verb form follows it.

> **Answers**
>
> 1 want that everything goes well → want everything to go well   2 feel like to watch → feel like watching   3 correct
> 4 meant to postpone → meant postponing   5 remember doing → remember to do   6 correct   7 go on to behave → go on behaving   8 regretted to not invite you → regretted not inviting / having invited you

Give students some further prompts to discuss in pairs. Encourage them to mention as many suggestions as possible using the target structures, rather than go into reasons in each case. Monitor pairs for accuracy. Write the following on the board or dictate them to the class.

Discuss things that you:

1 mustn't forget to do

2 regret (not) doing

3 have tried unsuccessfully to do

4 have tried doing but didn't enjoy

5 have been warned not to do

6 should be allowed to do

7 will always remember doing

8 keep meaning to do but never get round to doing

> **Suggested answers**
>
> 1 I mustn't forget to see that exhibition.
> 2 I regret losing that book.
> 3 I tried to learn the guitar, but gave up.
> 4 I once tried listening to that band but I found them boring.
> 5 We've been warned not to buy tickets over the Internet.
> 6 We should be allowed to take our own food into concerts.
> 7 I'll always remember seeing them live on stage.
> 8 I keeping meaning to watch an opera but I never get round to doing it.

See the Workbook and CD-ROM for further practice.

Reading and Use of English

Frequently confused words

1 Explain that in Reading and Use of English Part 1 some of the items depend on understanding the different meanings of the possible words, rather than on grammatical constraints, collocation, etc.

Let pairs use their dictionaries to work through this activity, making a note of vocabulary that is new to them together with suitable contexts. Point out that many of the options here are C1-level. When everyone has finished, go through the answers and distractors, eliciting examples with each.

> **Answers**
>
> 1 D   2 D   3 A   4 B   5 B   6 D

See the CD-ROM for further practice.

Part 1

2 Allow a minute for gist reading, then elicit answers.

> **Suggested answer**
>
> To say why contemporary art is important to individuals and society.

3 This can be done very quickly. Go through the answers and remind the class to check the parts of speech whenever they do this task type.

> **Answers**
>
> 1 verbs/present participles   2 adjectives   3 verbs   4 nouns
> 5 nouns   6 verbs   7 verbs   8 adverbs

4 Focus attention on the Quick steps and Exam tip, then give them ten minutes to do the exam task on their own. Check their answers and take any questions on the vocabulary in the text or options.

Exam task

> **Answers**
>
> 1 C   2 B   3 D   4 C   5 A   6 B   7 D   8 A

Listening

1 If necessary, give some background information on the objects shown [display from Barcelona Football Club; portrait photography exhibition from a school of photography; exhibition of posters of London Underground], but don't elicit vocabulary associated with each at this stage as they will do that in Exercise 3. Allow a couple of minutes for discussion in pairs and then ask the class for their impressions. Also ask why some people enjoy collecting fine-art photographs and/or posters/lithographs.

Part 4

2 Give the class 30 seconds to look at the instructions and questions, then elicit the answers.

> **Answers**
>
> Contexts in Task 1; feelings in Task 2.

3 Pairs brainstorm two or three words for each of A–H in both tasks. You may want to go quickly through these with the class after they finish, or leave it until after they have done the exam task.

4 🔊 *2.02* Focus attention on the Quick steps and the Exam tip, then play the recording right through without pausing. When it has finished, allow a few seconds for the class to check they have put an answer to every question. Replay the recording and then go through the answers.

If you wish, photocopy the script on page 76 for your students and ask them to underline the sections which give the answers.

Exam task

Answers
1 C 2 A 3 E 4 H 5 G 6 B 7 C 8 D 9 G 10 A

Recording script

Part 4 consists of two tasks. You will hear five short extracts in which people describe cultural activities.

Look at Task 1. For questions 1–5, choose from the list (A–H) the activity each speaker is describing.

Now look at Task 2. For questions 6–10, choose from the list (A–H) how each speaker says they felt during the activity.

While you listen you must complete both tasks. You now have 45 seconds to look at Part 4.

Speaker 1

Woman: Actually, I'd already seen the film version so there weren't any real plot surprises, but I was in one of the front rows and overall it was a reasonably enjoyable couple of hours. To be honest I wasn't expecting it to be up to much after what the critics had said about it, but at times <u>I found myself wondering whether they'd actually seen the same thing as me. How one of them could say,</u> for instance, that they felt 'thoroughly bored throughout' <u>remains a mystery to me.</u> In future I'll take a little less notice of the reviews, not just of <u>drama</u> but of exhibitions and opera, too.

Speaker 2

Man: There was certainly some rather clever photography, especially in the urban locations, and the <u>soundtrack</u> featuring some original songs was above average, too. But, as I'd read in a review somewhere, it was clear that the plot <u>lacked originality</u>, and before long the thought of having to put up with an entire <u>box set</u> of it <u>literally had me yawning</u>. My friends, though, seemed to find it quite absorbing so I had no option but to sit through the whole thing, wishing all the time I'd managed to persuade them to switch on that live broadcast of classical music instead.

Speaker 3

Woman: I was immediately struck by the craftsmanship, the skill and the dedication that must have gone into producing them. Some could have passed for photographs, they were that realistic, while others were so striking <u>I couldn't take my eyes off them</u>. That of course was why they'd been produced in the first place, from the time of the revolution and then up to and including the next great conflict. <u>I imagined them stuck on walls and in railways stations</u> as terrifying events took place, and could feel the immense power of the messages they must have conveyed at the time. I would have taken some photos but of course it isn't allowed there.

Speaker 4

Man: I'd gone along after seeing posters advertising the event, and I wasn't disappointed. Although <u>shot</u> in the so-called golden hour near the end of the day when <u>shadows</u> are softer, <u>the images shine a harsh light</u> on the reality of living in one of the most deprived parts of the country. Striking in their simplicity, and without accompanying notes as they speak for themselves, they capture the sense of <u>utter hopelessness</u> felt by people living in those conditions, leaving me with <u>much the same feeling. My spirits sank even further</u> when I thought about how little present-day society seems to care. We don't even make documentaries or films about them anymore.

Speaker 5

Woman: We'd been looking forward to our afternoon there, but it was <u>a real let-down, almost amateurish in fact</u>. There was an almost total lack of information, the facilities were poorly maintained and there were virtually no <u>exhibits</u> of any significance. A friendly but clueless member of staff explained that the most interesting <u>objects</u> were out on loan to the <u>archaeology</u> department of the university, and suggested we could see them being dug up in what he called 'the film'. This turned out to be a poor-quality video shown on an old TV, so we didn't bother. We might just have found all this amusing, but for the fact that we could have been at the theatre with friends instead.

See the Workbook for further practice.

Speaking

Expressing likes, dislikes & preferences

1 🔊 *2.03* Tell pairs to be careful with the structures used for some of these. Play the recording once right through, then again, pausing if and where necessary. Check everyone has the correct answers.

2 Point out that some of these appear in the dialogue in Exercise 1. Give pairs a minute to do this, then go through the answers and elicit an example of each. Suggest students make a note of them for future use, especially in Speaking Part 1.

3 Refer students to the Speaking Guide on page 107 either now or at the end of this section. Give pairs plenty of time to discuss these using expressions from Exercises 1 and 2. Tell them they can talk about any aspects of these cultural forms and/or the performers/artists themselves. If time allows, do a round-up at the end to see what the class's preferences are.

Part 1

4 2.04 Emphasise that they will only hear the final 30 seconds of each speaker doing Part 1. Tell the class to write the headings Olga and Nikos on a piece of paper, with the numbers 1–5 below each. Then, as they listen, they write *Yes* (Y), *No* (N), or *Possibly* (P) for each point. Play the recording, then elicit their answers and reasons. If you wish, photocopy the recording script on page 77 for the students. Ask them to listen again and check their answers.

5 2.04 Play the recording once or twice, allowing enough time for the expressions to be noted down. Elicit these, then ask for more ideas using these and other expressions from Exercises 1 and 2.

6 Focus attention on the Quick steps and Exam tip. Tell the 'examiners' to ask each 'candidate' two questions in sequence, and then do the same but choosing different questions with the other 'candidate'. Remind them of the importance of giving full answers. Make sure everyone starts and finishes at the same time, allowing about 30 seconds for each dialogue. Remind them to be sensitive and constructive in their comments.Refer students to page 107 of the Speaking guide.

Writing

Praising and criticising

1 Make sure everyone understands *criticise* and *praise*, and let them use dictionaries where necessary for the adjectives. Refer them back to the first page of this unit for some adverbs, but encourage them also to use others, as in the *Suggested answers* below. Go through these when pairs have finished.

2 Give students a minute or two to make notes, then tell them to work in pairs, using one expression for each film or series plus at least one adverb/adjective collocation to explain why. Monitor correct use of the infinitive or the

-ing form of the following verb. Elicit a few answers from the class.

Suggested answers

I would definitely recommend this film to anyone who likes romantic comedies.
My advice is not to waste your time watching this.
My advice is to see this as soon as you possibly can.
I would advise against watching this.
Viewers would be well advised to avoid this film.
This series is certainly worth trying.

Part 2: review

3 Point out that the Internet has made reviews much more accessible to more people, so pairs can consider more things than just the traditional books, films, plays, music, TV, etc. in the print media. Allow a couple of minutes for discussion, then elicit some answers to the three questions.

Suggested answers

1 Newspapers and magazines: books, films, plays, concerts, albums, singles, exhibitions, shows, TV programmes. Online: almost anything where there is consumer choice, from hoovers to hotels.
2 A brief description of the product, service or form of entertainment, praise and/or criticism, recommendation or not.

4 Allow 30 seconds for the class to look at the exam task, then go through the answers. Suggest they ask themselves questions like these whenever they are about to do a review task.

Answers

1 Two films of a similar type, e.g. action, comedy, old or new.
2 A film review website. To help film lovers make informed choices about which films to watch.
3 Review two films of a similar type, compare and contrast them, and make recommendations.

5 Give the class a minute or two to gist read the text, noting down their answers as they do so. Then ask the class what they think.

Answers

1 a) in general, yes   b) in general, yes   2 Skyfall

6 Explain or elicit the meaning of *synopsis*. Allow plenty of time for pairs to study the text, then go through the answers. Take any questions on vocabulary in the text, and highlight useful expressions such as *action film, superbly-shot locations, pace, viewer's attention, highly-accomplished actors, title songs, suspense building music, brilliantly played.*

Answers

1 synopsis in 2, recommendations in 5, background information in 1, characters in 2 & 3, reader's attention in 1 (and title), criticises in 4, praises in 1, 3 & 5.
2 Similarities: both very popular James Bond action films; both set in a variety of locations; pace holds the viewer's attention; good actors playing Bond; title songs, incidental music; car; scary opponents; role of women remains the same.
Contrasts: made 50 years apart; different directors and actors playing Bond; different places & villains; different focus of the attack; villain's assistant in *Goldfinger* notable, but *Skyfall* more exciting because of long action sequences. Bond's boss is a woman in *Skyfall*. *Skyfall* criticised for its violence.
3 massively-popular, aptly-named, superbly-shot, utterly evil, highly-accomplished, genuinely scary, rather unnecessary
4 neutral/fairly formal
5 … are certainly worth watching; I would probably recommend
6 Students' own answers

7 Read through the Quick steps with the students. Allow them less than a minute to look at the exam task, then elicit the answers.

Answers

1 two different TV series
2 in an international magazine called *Home Entertainment*, to help readers choose box sets of TV series
3 compare and contrast the two series

8 Elicit different types of TV series, e.g. comedy, detective, cartoon, etc. Give groups a few minutes to brainstorm ideas. Elicit some answers to the questions.

9 Tell the class to treat these points as possible prompts, as they don't need all this information for a short review. Students work on their own, noting down points to include and then putting them into suitable paragraphs. Allow at least five minutes for this.Remind students they can refer to page 105 of the Writing guide.

10 Give the class 35 minutes for the writing, as they have already studied the task and planned their review. Remind them to leave plenty of time at the end for checking.

Model answer

Two unmissable TV series

Downton Abbey and *Sherlock* are two hugely popular fiction series that have received numerous awards in various countries.

In both cases the writing, directing, acting, photography and music have been critically acclaimed, although they are quite different programmes. While *Sherlock* focuses primarily on the detectives Holmes and Watson, *Downton Abbey* is about the lives of a large aristocratic family and their servants. Interestingly, it was written recently but is set in the early twentieth century, whereas *Sherlock* is based on books written around that time but updated to a present-day setting.

The two series succeed in maintaining the viewer's interest and creating suspense in different ways. Each *Sherlock* story has a single complex plot, while in *Downton* there are compelling interlinked storylines. The latter is also set against an interesting historical background of events such as the sinking of the *Titanic*. *Sherlock*, on the other hand, will particularly appeal to those who enjoy trying to solve the case before the detective.

Some, however, may dislike the rather cold, arrogant personality of Holmes. In contrast, the larger cast in *Downtown* includes likeable characters such as Violet Crawley, brilliantly played by Maggie Smith. Others though may feel that it romanticises situations of extreme social inequality, or simply be tired of costume dramas.

Nevertheless, I would recommend both series. Viewers who like visually spectacular programmes with a range of believable characters and a touch of romance would undoubtedly enjoy *Downton*, while anyone who appreciates depth of characterisation and fascinating, intricate plots should order their box set of *Sherlock* immediately.

See the Workbook and CD-ROM for further practice.

7 Green issues

Unit objectives

TOPICS	nature & the environment
GRAMMAR	inversion after negative adverbials
VOCABULARY	collocations; phrasal verbs with *on* idioms: nature
READING AND USE OF ENGLISH	Part 4: key word transformations; Part 7: gapped text
WRITING	Part 1 essay: sentence adverbs, paraphrasing notes
LISTENING	Part 1: short texts, multiple-choice questions
SPEAKING	Part 3: giving examples, helping your partner

Listening

Collocations

1 Give pairs a couple of minutes to talk, then ask the class for some of their thoughts. The photos (from left to right) were taken in a tropical rainforest in Khao Yai National Park in Thailand; the Bernese Alps in Switzerland; the English Lake District.

2 🔘 2.05 Tell pairs they can use dictionaries for this. After a few minutes, play the recording to check their answers.

Answers

1 carbon emissions   2 fossil fuels   3 rainforest clearance
4 forest fires   5 global warming   6 climate change
7 drought conditions   8 melting ice caps
9 rising sea–levels   10 habitat destruction
11 endangered species   12 become extinct

Recording script

With rising carbon emissions caused by the widespread use of fossil fuels, as well as extensive rainforest clearance and increasingly frequent forest fires, it is hardly surprising that global warming, also called climate change, is quickening its pace. Its damaging effects range from drought conditions in warmer countries to melting ice caps in the Polar regions, and rising sea-levels around the world. For wildlife, these changes can lead to habitat destruction, increasing the number of endangered species – with the risk that some will eventually become extinct.

3 Tell pairs to consider the issues raised in the text vis-a-vis each of the three types of landscape and vegetation. Allow about five minutes for this, then elicit some answers.

Suggested answers

Rainforest: 1 Vital for absorbing CO_2 from atmosphere, holding moisture, habitat for huge variety of plants and animals.
2 Threatened by clearance leading to permanent loss of trees, animal habitats, undergrowth.

Alpine: 1 Important for climate cooling & precipitation, as a water resource, habitat for alpine flora and fauna, etc. 2 Higher temperatures can melt ice/snow, lower rainfall/snow can lead to reduced snow cover, rivers and streams drying up, soil erosion, loss of flora & fauna.

Temperate: 1 Forests absorb CO_2, lakes and rivers provide water resources, vegetation provides habitat for wide range of animals. 2 Land being urbanised, rivers and air being polluted, rising temperatures affecting flora & fauna, rising sea-levels submerging coastal areas.

See the Workbook and CD-ROM for further practice.

Part 1

4 Remind the class that in the exam there will not be photos, nor will there be any thematic link between the extracts as here. Give pairs a few minutes to note down their answers, including underlining the key words if you don't mind them writing in the book.

Answers

1 1 alpine scene (middle photo) 2 rainforest (first photo)
  3 temperate countryside (last photo)
2 1 two colleagues; the man's recent holiday   2 two friends; a
  documentary about a tropical rainforest   3 Anne Murphy and
  an interviewer; a campaign against building a new factory.
3 1 what, man, complain   2 how, woman, react   3 agree
  4 man, programme, seemed, made   5 opposed, because
  6 prefer, plan

5 🔘 2.06 Focus attention on the Quick steps and the Exam tip, then play the recording through without pausing. Allow a little time for everyone to check they have put an answer to every question, then go through the answers.

If you wish, photocopy the script on page 78 for your students and ask them to underline the sections which give answers.

Exam task

Answers

1 B   2 A   3 A   4 B   5 C   6 A

Recording script

You'll hear three different extracts. For questions 1–6, choose the answer (A, B or C) which fits best according to what you hear. There are two questions for each extract.

Extract One

You overhear two colleagues talking about the man's recent holiday.

Now look at questions one and two.

M: Higher up on the main slopes there was far less than in previous years; in fact there were huge bare patches on some of them. It must have put a lot of other people off, too. The whole resort area is usually quite crowded but this time there was hardly a soul in sight, even though all the hotel prices were heavily discounted. So all in all it was something of a wasted trip, really.

F: Well, I think I'd have counted myself lucky just to be somewhere that beautiful at this time of year! But if what you saw there is part of a more general pattern, and it does seem the same thing's been happening in mountainous areas in other parts of the world, then it looks as though we're seeing the physical results of climate change sooner than we expected even just a few years ago.

M: Or maybe it's just a temporary thing, as some people claim. Periods of warm and cold weather go in cycles, don't they?

F: To some extent, certainly. But I think we're looking at a longer-term trend now.

Extract Two

You hear two friends discussing a documentary programme about a tropical rainforest.

Now look at questions three and four.

F: It was over-ambitious, really, wasn't it? I mean, trying to pack into 40 minutes the entire evolution of the rainforests, the range of trees, plants and animals in them, plus all the danger they're now in. It's just not possible.

M: I don't think I could have sat through any more of that, to be honest. Especially with the narrator talking to viewers as if they were schoolkids. It was like being back in biology lessons. He sounded like he'd never done a voice-over before.

F: Actually, I thought he had quite a pleasant voice, though I must admit I could have done without it whenever I was trying to listen to all those marvellous background sounds: the birds and monkeys and everything.

M: I've seen better camera work, too. At times that looked more like a home video.

F: There were some nice shots, though. Especially those taken from above the tree tops.

M: Yes, they were very much the exceptions, and they must've paid some actual professionals quite a lot to get those. Though they could have saved all that money by filming it in Cairns, in north-east Australia. There's a cable car near there that runs right above the rainforest.

Extract Three

You hear part of an interview with a woman called Anne Murphy, who is campaigning against the building of a new factory.

Now look at questions five and six.

Int: Anne, can you tell us why you're so opposed to this scheme?

Anne: Quite simply it's a local beauty spot, and whoever had the idea of putting a food processing factory in those lovely green fields right next to the river simply doesn't care how much damage it would do. I know the plan includes an effective water treatment plant, but such a large development would be impossible without new roads, power lines and so on, with all the harm that would do to the countryside.

Int: And what do the farmers say about this?

Anne: Well, there's a lot of compensation on offer and they're likely to take it. Actually, they've now said that if this scheme doesn't go ahead they'll find another buyer for the land, so doing nothing with it isn't an option, either. Finding an alternative use for it, perhaps as a country park or something like that, sounds like the best bet. I know that some of the people on the town council have argued for going ahead with the plan on a slightly reduced scale, but that's completely out of the question as far as I'm concerned.

See the Workbook and CD-ROM for further practice.

Grammar

Inversion of subject and verb

1 Give pairs plenty of time to do both parts of this exercise, letting them check with the Grammar reference on page 95 where necessary. Go through the answers to 1–12 and a–f.

If your students are likely to be unfamiliar with these forms, spend more time on the first part of Exercise 1 by asking them to rewrite 1–12 without inversion, once they have corrected the mistakes. This will enable them to see more clearly the changes required for inversion.

> **Answers**
>
> **1** correct   **2** correct   **3** they will discover → will they discover   **4** correct   **5** Sonia had ever had → had Sonia ever had   **6** we can allow → can we allow   **7** correct   **8** correct **9** correct   **10** did he finished → had he finished **11** correct   **12** Not only private cars contribute → Not only do private cars contribute
>
> **a** Adverbials with a negative or limiting meaning.   **b** At the beginning (or the beginning of a clause).   **c** It sounds more emphatic/dramatic.   **d** The auxiliary precedes the subject. **e** The correct form of *do*.   **f** Usually only in formal writing, or formal speeches.

> **Answers (sentences without inversion)**
>
> **1** I have seldom seen …   **2** The children had little idea … **3** They will only discover any hidden talents they might have when they start performing.   **4** Travelling did not become a widespread phenomenon until the 20th century.   **5** Sonia had never before had …   **6** We cannot, under any circumstances, allow …   **7** We should not, on any account, assume … **8** He had hardly finished when …   **9** When she was in Paris, Carlota was not really aware of her true feelings at any time. **10** He had no sooner finished his studies than …   **11** You won't see this strange-sounding but lovely bird anywhere else in the world.   **12** Private cars not only contribute …

2 Students do these on their own. Check their work for accuracy.

Answers

1 Only when we arrived in Kenya did we see hippos and giraffes. **2** Hardly had I unpacked in my hotel room when my phone rang. **3** Seldom do the nature reserve guards catch illegal hunters. **4** Never before have I seen such a spectacular waterfall. **5** No longer are there any tigers in the northern region. **6** No sooner had the zebras entered the water than hungry crocodiles appeared. **7** On no account must visitors to the forest light fires. **8** In no way are the local people to blame for the destruction of the forest.

3 Tell students they can choose any suitable structures for these, as long as they involve subject/verb inversion. When they have finished, either check their written work and/or elicit answers from the class.

Suggested answers

1 Never before has there been such a long drought. **2** Little did we know what would happen when darkness fell. **3** Not until the storm has passed will there be any chance of rescuing survivors. **4** On no account are visitors permitted to leave the designated footpaths. **5** Not only are there bears in those hills, there are also wolves. **6** No sooner had the rains come than wild flowers started to appear. **7** Rarely do you see fish in a river as polluted as this. **8** Hardly had the climbers set off for the summit when it began to snow.

4 Students do this on their own. Make it clear that they only have to write three sentences for each of 1–4, not a whole text. Check their written work for accuracy.

Suggested answers

1. must you swim in the river; should you leave your vehicle; can you feed the animals.
2. had I left the house when I heard footsteps behind me; had I started calling when the line went dead; did I expect the journey to be so difficult.
3. will you see such wonderful forests; can you find so many species of butterfly; are there such lovely beaches.
4. the 19th century did it become independent; the railway lines were built did it become possible to travel easily; the last century have so many people been out of work.

See the Workbook and CD-ROM for further practice.

Reading and Use of English

Part 7

1 Elicit the meanings of these mainly C1-level expressions, then give pairs a couple of minutes to discuss the pictures. Encourage them to use the skills they have acquired from Speaking Part 2 to compare and contrast the scenes, and imagine the sounds and smells. The photos were taken in Japan, Thailand and the U.S.

Suggested answers

Although the first photo is in a large city, the traffic is very light. The road is very wide with four lanes and the traffic is free-flowing. It looks like a business district with lots of offices but it can't be rush hour.

The second photo is also in a city but much busier. The road has three lanes but it doesn't seem to be as well ordered as the first photo. For example, I can't see any lane markings. It's probably rush hour. I wouldn't like to be on the motorbike as the exhaust fumes must be quite bad. It also could be quite noisy with drivers blowing their car horns trying to get people to move out of their way. Traffic jams must be common at certain times of the day here.

There are different types of vehicles in this photo including private cars, taxis and buses. However, in the third picture, there are mainly private cars, although I can see a few taxis. I suspect the drivers are mainly commuters trying to get to or from work but it will take them a long time because the road is in gridlock. All the cars are quite big so the fuel consumption must be high. I can't see clearly but I don't think the car occupancy will be high. I think they should introduce a law to stop cars with only one person from using the roads at certain times of day. The pollution here must be terrible and it must take ages to go anywhere! I'd hate to live anywhere where the congestion on the roads was that bad.

2 Tell pairs the third point relates directly to the exam task to follow. Give them two or three minutes to discuss, but only go through the answers to 1 and 2 as answering the third question will give them a reason to gist read the exam text.

3 Remind the class, working individually, to skim read the text and missing paragraphs, not read every word. Elicit the answers to questions 1 and 3, but not 2. These will vary from student to student, and detail is not required at this stage. The answers to 1 and 3, on the other hand, will be useful to them when they do the task, so ask the class what they think. Ask students to give an explanation of the expression 'end of the road' (the moment when someone or something has to stop, for example because they cannot succeed or improve).

Answers

1 car-crazy culture **3** Discursive, i.e. it develops an argument. Addition links, contrast links, reference words, synonyms and near-synonyms.

4 Point out that the clues are given as a way of raising awareness of the kind of cohesive devices they need to be looking for in this kind of task. Draw attention to the Quick steps and the Exam tip, then give the class 12–15 minutes to do the exam task, working on their own. When they have finished, remind them to check they have answered all the questions, then go through the answers. If there is time, also look at the clues in more detail.

Answers

1 1 the high point of the car; that peak; The phenomenon
3 rise of 'virtual commuters'; these new employment patterns
4 car boom; less green trends **6** unexpectedly going up; miscalulations; these trends
2 may be a factor. And urban gridlock; ... a dumb way
3 Besides
4 Likewise; But

Exam task

> **Answers**
>
> 1 F   2 B   3 G   4 A   5 E   6 C

> See the Workbook and CD-ROM for further practice.

5 Give students, working individually, two minutes to note down their answers. Go through these, eliciting more example sentences with each phrasal verb, including other meanings such as *go on* = continue, *rely on* = trust.

> **Answers**
>
> carry on: continue doing (also continue)
> go on: happen (also continue)
> rely on: use/need/depend on (also trust)
> look on: consider in a particular way (also watch but not become involved)
> insist on: keep doing something even if it is not a good idea (also demand to have something)

Speaking

Phrasal verbs with *on*

1 Pairs do these in two or three minutes. Check their answers and elicit more examples with some or all of the phrasal verbs.

> **Answers**
>
> 1 stayed on   2 draws on   3 catch on   4 taken/taking on
> 5 comes on   6 called on   7 runs on   8 move on

Giving examples

2 ● 2.07 Point out that there are other common ways of giving examples apart from saying *for instance, for example* or *such as*, particularly in spoken language. Give pairs a minute or two to attempt to fill in the gaps, possibly giving them some help by telling them that three of the words they need are verbs in the imperative form. Play the recording and check their answers, explaining that there are various phrases possible with 4, e.g. *a good ..., a well-known ... .*

> **Answers**
>
> 1 Look   2 say   3 point   4 example   5 take

> **Recording script**
>
> Environmentalists are calling on all of us to recognise that waste is fast becoming a major problem. Look at the amount we throw out every year. A family of three, say, produces more than a ton of rubbish every year, and this is steadily rising. A case in point is plastic, used in ever greater quantities and often ending up in the bin. An obvious example of this is the plastic shopping bag. Also, take paper waste. Did you know that every year the average family throws out the equivalent of six trees?

3 Students can work in pairs. Give them an example, e.g. *Take the amount of good food thrown out by supermarkets ...*, and encourage them to discuss each point briefly before moving on to the next example, using the expressions from Exercise 2. Tell them to avoid suggesting solutions at this stage, as the focus of Speaking Part 3 will be ways of reducing the amount of waste we create.

Part 3

4 Give pairs a minute to look at the task, then elicit the answer.

> **Answers**
>
> Suggestions for reducing the amount of waste we create

5 ● 2.08 Make it clear that they will hear a short extract, not the whole task. Play the recording once through without pausing, then ask the class for the answer. If you wish, photocopy the recording script on page 79 for the students. Ask them to listen again and check their answers.

> **Answers**
>
> 1 Give away unwanted clothes   2 Haziq, the man

> **Recording script**
>
> | Aishar: | <u>So how do you feel about this one?</u> |
> | Haziq: | I think it's a good idea. |
> | Aishar: | <u>Any particular reason?</u> |
> | Haziq: | Well, a lot of people throw out clothes they've only worn a couple of times, which is a terrible waste. |
> | Aishar: | <u>That's a good point.</u> |
> | Haziq: | So instead of doing that they could put them, say, in one of those things you see in the street for used clothes. |
> | Aishar: | <u>Right, I know the ones you mean.</u> Or you could take them to a charity shop, Oxfam for instance, who sell them to raise money. Either way someone gets to wear them, free or at a lower price. |
> | Haziq: | Yes, and that means they don't become waste. |
> | Aishar: | OK, the next one. <u>What are your thoughts on this?</u> |

6 ● 2.08 Play the recording once or twice more, pausing if necessary for students to make notes. Go through the answers, suggesting they use some of these expressions when they do the task themselves. Refer them also to page 109 of the Speaking guide.

> **Answers**
>
> So how do you feel about this one?
> Any particular reason?   That's a good point.
> Right, I know the ones you mean.
> What are your thoughts on this?

7 Go through any questions raised by the Quick steps or Exam tip. Time the activity so that it lasts no longer than three minutes in total (you may want to indicate when the first two minutes are up).

8 When they have finished, ask pairs which suggestions they chose as the most effective, with brief reasons. Ask the class if they can come up with more ideas, such as buying reusable products, refusing to accept free plastic bags in supermarkets, recycling old mobile phones and computers, etc.

Reading and Use of English

Idioms: nature

1 Encourage pairs to work out the idiomatic meanings for themselves, but let them use dictionaries for any they find difficult. Go through the answers, asking about similar ones in their first language(s) and checking that they do in fact have the same meaning.

> **Answers**
>
> 1 f 2 h 3 g 4 c 5 d 6 b 7 a 8 e

2 Give pairs a minute or two to do these, then go through the answers.

> **Answers**
>
> 1 over the moon 2 playing with fire 3 to keep your head above water 4 a drop in the ocean 5 out of the blue 6 down to earth 7 the tip of the iceberg 8 a breath of fresh air

For extra practice, students work in pairs to give examples of the following using the idioms:

1 something which happened out of the blue

2 someone you know who is down to earth

3 a social problem that is only the tip of the iceberg

4 something new that is a breath of fresh air

5 a situation in which some people play with fire

6 an occasion when you were over the moon

Monitor and help as they are working. Choose students to tell the rest of the class an example answer.

Part 4

3 Read through the Quick steps with the students then allow a minute at most for the exercise. Quickly check the answers without going into any detail.

> **Answers**
>
> a) 2
> b) 4 & 6
> c) 1, 3 & 5

4 Students work on these on their own for about 12 minutes. They should find the preparation they have done helpful, but remind them that they will not have these clues in the exam. Point out that the idioms tested here have not already been introduced in this Unit. Draw attention to the Exam tip. Make sure they haven't given more than one answer and then check the answers.

Exam task

> **Answers**
>
> 1 sooner had the storm begun | than 2 to | catch on with
> 3 circumstances | should visitors approach 4 lost track | of
> (the) 5 only do | those trucks pollute 6 unsuccessfully | to
> break the ice

Writing

Sentence adverbs

1 Give an example or two of how sentence adverbs are used, e.g. *I knew they were in when I rang the bell. Strangely, nobody came to the door.* Explain that they are often used in writing to emphasise particular points or events. Then tell pairs to do the exercise, if necessary using their dictionaries for some of the adverbs. Go through the answers when they have finished, and elicit more adverbs commonly used in this way, e.g. *amazingly*, *curiously*, *predictably*, plus adverbial phrases such as *of course* or *at least*.

> **Answers**
>
> 1 unexpectedly. 2 , generally 3 Apparently, 4 , sadly.
> 5 Fortunately, 6 Unsurprisingly, 7 happily 8 , admittedly,
> 9 Obviously, 10 Mysteriously,

2 Point out that in some cases more than one answer is possible, as attitudes are bound to vary. Tell students to work on their own, though they can compare their completed sentences with their partners if they wish. Check their work and elicit some answers.

> **Suggested answers**
>
> 1 Apparently, summers are going to get hotter.
> 2 Fortunately / Happily etc, someone found it and gave it back to me.
> 3 Unsurprisingly / Sadly / Unexpectedly etc, most said 'no'.
> 4 I failed my biology exam but admittedly I hadn't done enough revision.
> 5 I looked round, but mysteriously there was no-one there.
> 6 Unexpectedly, s/he knocked on my door.

> See the Workbook for further practice.

Part 1: essay

3 For questions 1 & 2, groups may be able to work these out by a process of elimination, but if not they can use dictionaries for further clues. Encourage the use of sentence adverbs such as *obviously* and *apparently*.

For question 3, emphasise that 'creatures' covers not only mammals but also birds, fish, reptiles, amphibians, insects, etc, and that they can be from anywhere in the world. Allow a couple of minutes for this and then elicit answers.

For question 4, remind students that some of these points may be useful when they come to write their essay. Give the class two or three minutes to do this, and then elicit some answers.

> **Answers**
>
> 1 & 2 A Snow leopard – Asia B Vicuna – S America C Black Rhinoceros – Africa D Southern water vole – Europe
> 3 (Suggested answers) Certain types of gorilla, turtle and seal; giant panda, blue whale, African penguin, Asian elephant, etc.
> 4 (Suggested answers) Loss of habitat owing to development, use of pesticides, climate change affecting temperatures and rainfall patterns, invasive species, diseases, hunting, etc.

4 Give the class a minute to look at the task and elicit the answers. Leave the three opinions for Exercise 5.

> **Answers**
>
> **1** How governments around the world should help protect endangered species; for your tutor.
> **2** education, protected zones, legislation
> **3** Say which you think would be more effective, giving reasons.

5 Draw attention to *you should use your own words as far as possible* in the instructions, and point out that although students can use the odd word or phrase from the *opinions expressed*, they should always try to change the wording wherever they can, and add to the ideas they express. Give the class, working on their own, a minute or two to decide on their answers. With a strong class, ask them to think of other ways of paraphrasing each of the opinions.

> **Answers**
>
> **1** A too similar to the original   B best   C oversimplified
> **2** A best   B oversimplified   C too similar to the original
> **3** A oversimplified   B too similar to the original   C best

6 Give pairs five minutes to study the text and note down their answers. Take any vocabulary questions as you go through the answers.

> **Answers**
>
> **1** protected zones 3rd paragraph; legislation 2nd paragraph
> **2** "It ought to be illegal ..." → *One solution is to pass strict laws* ...; 2nd paragraph
>   "We can help endangered ..." → *create protected zones, where* ...; 3rd paragraph
> **3** Legislation, because there are not enough resources to establish protected zones for all the animals at risk, but laws can be applied globally.
> **4** Inversion: At no time in recorded history have so many species; Not only must the hunting or capturing of endangered or threatened species be made.
>   Sentence adverbs: Alarmingly; Clearly; Crucially; Unfortunately; undeniably,
>   Addition links: Not only...also; In addition; Another
>   Contrast links: but; however; on the other hand

7 Students brainstorm these points on their own for four to five minutes. Encourage them also to come up with their own ideas.

8 Allow 35 minutes for the actual writing, as they are already familiar with the task and have made notes for their essay. Then give them five minutes for checking, possibly in pairs. Remind them to check the Writing guide on page 99 before they start writing as well.

Model answer

Never before have so many different kinds of creature been threatened with extinction by human activity. Tragically, many species have already disappeared, and unless urgent action is taken many more will be lost to this planet forever. The disaster is on such a scale that governments everywhere must act immediately.

They should do so, firstly, by passing strictly-enforced laws banning not only the harming of endangered or threatened species, but also any damage to their habitats, the plants they feed on and any other creatures they depend on within the food chain. Hunting and fishing for sport should also be outlawed, as should the transportation of invasive species between countries. The killing or smuggling of species at risk, plus the trade in products from those creatures, must be punished severely.

Secondly, all citizens need to be made aware of the extent of the crisis, its consequences for the world, and what they can do to help. This should begin at school, with all children taught to respect animal life and shown how to take part in local conservation schemes. Also, wildlife documentaries and films could inform adults about the main issues, such as the direct and indirect impact of climate change on animals. The latter includes the increased incidence of wildfires, desertification, and flooding caused by rising sea levels.

Unfortunately, however, education takes time to bring about change. Suitable legislation, in contrast, could quickly transform the situation, which is why I believe that international treaties committing all governments to the measures outlined above would be the more effective strategy.

> See the Workbook for further practice.

8 Learning and working

Unit objectives

TOPICS	education, learning & work
GRAMMAR	relative clauses; introductory *it/what*
VOCABULARY	affixes; spelling changes
READING AND	Part 3: word formation;
USE OF ENGLISH	Part 8: multiple matching
WRITING	Part 2 letter: formal language, text organisation
LISTENING	Part 2: sentence completion
SPEAKING	Part 4: adding emphasis, hedging

Reading and Use of English

Part 8

1 Give pairs a few minutes to do these, with the help of dictionaries if necessary, and then go through the answers with the class.

> **Answers**
>
> 1 a) the process of getting knowledge or a new skill
> b) the activity of teaching or training someone
> 2 a) a formal talk given to a group of people, especially students
> b) a period of study with a tutor involving one student or a small group
> 3 a) someone who teaches at a college or university
> b) teacher of the highest rank in a department of a university
> 4 a) person who studies a subject in great detail, especially at a university
> b) serious, detailed study OR money given by a school, college, university, etc. to pay for the studies of a person
> 5 a) discussion involving a teacher or expert and a group of people
> b) meeting involving practical work in a subject or activity
> 6 a) put your name down for a course, college, etc.
> b) successfully finish a course so that you are able to do a job
> 7 a) a person who has a first degree from a university OR to complete a degree course successfully
> b) finishing a degree at a university or school OR the ceremony at which degree certificates are awarded
> 8 a) student studying for their first degree at university
> b) student who already has one degree and is studying at university for a more advanced qualification
> 9 a) having learned a lot at school or university and having a good level of knowledge
> b) providing education or relating to education
> a) document giving details of a school, university or business and its activities
> 10 b) subjects or books to be studied in a particular course, especially a course that leads to an exam

2 Pairs discuss these points for two or three minutes. After they finish, ask the class for some of their answers. Make sure they understand what each of the activities shown involves.

> **Suggested answers**
>
> 1 attending a lecture, attending a tutorial, taking part in a group activity, self-study
> 2 Students' own answers
> 3 learning by doing a particular task, learning from friends or relatives, online learning

3 Give the class, working on their own, no more than a minute or two to skim the text and form an impression of each learning style. Tell them not to worry about understanding particular words or phrases at this stage. Ask a few students which section or sections (if they think more than one applies to them) they have chosen and to explain – very briefly – why.

4 Draw attention to the Quick steps and Exam tip, then give the class, working on their own, 12–15 minutes to do the underlining and the exam task. Go through the answers, but leave any language queries until after they have done Exercise 5.

For your information, the definitions of the learner are taken from Honey, P. & Mumford, A. (1982) Manual of Learning Styles, London. The person who prefers style A in the task is described as the Theorist, B as the Pragmatist, C as the Activist and D as the Reflector. You may want to tell your class this.

Exam task

> **Answers**
>
> 1 D 2 C 3 A 4 B 5 B 6 D 7 A 8 C 9 B 10 D

5 Give pairs a few minutes to do this exercise, referring to dictionaries if necessary but wherever possible using the context. Go through the answers, eliciting more examples of some or all of them in other contexts.

> **Answers**
>
> 1 will not be satisfied 2 the subject being considered
> 3 completely full of 4 having no set limit 5 keep doing or talking about the same thing without achieving anything
> 6 become quieter 7 experienced yourself 8 consider the facts and decide what is true, correct, etc. 9 the most important thing 10 choose not to be in a position of responsibility
> 11 understand the general meaning of what someone is saying 12 avoid attracting attention to oneself

See the Workbook and CD-ROM for further practice.

Grammar

Relative clauses

1 Give pairs plenty of time to correct the errors and discuss why they are wrong, then go through the answers with the class. Refer students to the Grammar reference on page 95 if necessary.

Answers

1 You, who: *that* is not used in a non-defining relative clause
2 when I have: we use *when* as a relative pronoun for time references
3 who were not: *who* is the subject of the verb 'were' so 'they' is not needed
4 which seems: *what* means 'the thing that', which would not make sense here
5 whose work: the possessive relative pronoun is *whose*; *who's* means 'who is' or 'who has'
6 where you are: *where* is used as a relative pronoun for place references
7 whose ages: *whose* is the possessive relative pronoun
8 course, which: non-defining relative clause; there is only one Business English course
9 who are refusing: *who* is the relative pronoun for people in non-defining relative clauses
10 which took place: *that* is not used in a non-defining relative clause

2 Give pairs two or three minutes to complete the exercise. Point out that there may be more than one reason why a relative pronoun can or cannot be omitted, but they only need identify one. Go through the answers, possibly eliciting more examples with and without omission.

Answers

1 My younger brother showed me the essay which / that he had written.
2 That's the primary school where I met my best friend.
3 On Sundays, when the library is closed, I read at home.
4 Students whose parents have a low income can apply for a grant.
5 The teacher who / that I liked most was Mr Anderson.
6 Maths, which was my favourite subject, was our first lesson of the day.
7 My mother, who is a lecturer, did her PhD at Cambridge.
8 The college which / that I studied at has since closed.

1 Omission possible because *which/that* is the object in its clause.
2 Omission not possible with *where*.
3 Omission not possible with *when*.
4 Omission not possible with *whose*.
5 Omission possible because *who/that* is the object in its clause.
6 Omission not possible in non-defining relative clause.
7 Omission not possible in non-defining relative clause.
8 Omission possible because *which/that* is the object in its clause.

3 Ask whether this form is common in the students' language(s), and explain that in formal written or spoken English, prepositions are sometimes placed before *which* and *whom*. Give a few more examples then get pairs to rewrite the sentences, adding the omitted *which* or replacing the omitted *who* with *whom*. Check their answers and elicit more examples with a variety of prepositions.

Answers

1 The research on which the theory is based is unreliable.
2 The people with whom Stephen studied with were all experts.
3 We were shown the desk at which the President sits.
4 There is an Open Day to which prospective students are invited.
5 He is a philosopher about whom many books been written.
6 The day on which the Queen was born was a Friday.
7 That distant star has a planet about which we know little.
8 The person to whom I wrote has yet to reply.

4 If the class are unfamiliar with these forms, give some more examples with both *which* and *whom*. You can also refer them to the Grammar reference on page 95. Allow a couple of minutes to do the exercise, then go through the answers.

Answers

1 I have two sisters, both of whom are at university.
2 Nicky sent off two job applications, neither of which was successful.
3 I've lost touch with most of my ex-classmates, many of whom went abroad to study.
4 This department has done a lot of research, all of which has been published.
5 Astronomers observed a large number of meteorities, few of which reached the ground.
6 In the study we interviewed hundreds of people, the majority of whom lived locally.
7 This is where the ancient city stood, little of which remains today.
8 The talk was attended by a large audience, none of whom left before the end.

See the Workbook and CD-ROM for further practice.

Reading and Use of English

Words with a prefix and a suffix

1 Point out that there may be a mistake in either the prefix or the suffix, and that there may be more than one possible base word – either which could be the word given in a Reading and Use of English Part 3 task. Allow pairs a couple of minutes to do the exercise, then check their answers.

Answers

1 inescapable – escape 2 illegally – legal 3 dissatisfaction – satisfy 4 overprotective – protect 5 Undeniably – deny, deniable 6 upbringing – bring 7 inexplicably – explain, explicable 8 indescribable – describe

If you wish to give students more practice in words with a prefix and suffix, give them a few words now and then to practise with. Get them to give the new word and the part of speech, for example: profession – professional (adj); person – impersonal (adj); signify – insignificant (adj); think – unthinkable (adj); able – inability (noun); approve – disapproval (noun); help – unhelpful (adj); accurate – inaccuracies (plural noun)

See the CD-ROM for further practice.

Spelling changes

2 Allow pairs to use dictionaries for words such as *detain* and *resolve*. After two or three minutes, go through the answers, checking for spelling accuracy.

> **Answers**
>
> **1** proof   **2** deepened   **3** strengthen   **4** maintenance
> **5** breadth   **6** resolution   **7** repetition   **8** detention

> See the Workbook and CD-ROM for further practice.

Part 3

3 Refer students to the Quick steps. Give the class a minute to do this gist-reading task and then elicit the answers.

> **Answers**
>
> **1** The abilities and experience they will need in the actual workplace.
> **2** Students' own answers

4 Tell the class to do the exam task on their own, in no more than ten minutes. After they finish and you have gone through the answers, get them to identify the words that required both a prefix and a suffix, and those that needed internal spelling changes.

Exam task

> **Answers**
>
> **1** uncertainty   **2** increasingly   **3** capability   **4** prospective
> **5** advisors / advisers   **6** theoretical   **7** ensuring
> **8** unwillingness
> *Both a prefix and a suffix*: uncertainty, ensuring, unwillingness
> *Internal spelling changes*: capability, advisors, theoretical

Listening

Part 2

1 Give groups plenty of time to categorise these mostly C1-level verbs and phrases, using dictionaries where necessary. Point out that a few are more common in either the UK or the US. Go through the answers, eliciting any differences in meaning.

> **Answers**
>
> **a)** get or do a job: go into, be employed, practise, serve, hold down a job
> **b)** give somebody a job: hire, recruit, take on, fill a position, appoint
> **c)** leave a job: quit, resign, retire, step down
> **d)** make somebody leave a job: dismiss, fire, lay off, make redundant, sack, let go
> **e)** without a job: out of a job, on benefits
>
> **a)** go into a profession; practise law / medicine, etc.; serve in the army / as mayor, etc.; hold down a job with difficulty
> **b)** hire (US); fill a position, i.e. when there is a vacancy
> **c)** retire when old; step down from a position of responsibility
> **d)** dismiss / fire (US) / sack (UK) for misconduct, etc.
> **e)** on benefits (UK) – receiving state benefits because, e.g., you are unemployed or disabled

2 Point out that the main aim of this activity is to practise language from Exercise 1. Allow two or three minutes for this, then ask the class for their answers.

3 Explain that this is the topic of the Listening text to follow. Give pairs a minute or two to discuss these points but don't go through the answers.

4 Individuals or pairs look quickly through the questions. You may want to check their answers now, or leave it until after they do the exam task.

> **Answers**
>
> **1** noun   **2** adjective   **3** noun   **4** number   **5** noun   **6** noun
> **7** number   **8** noun/phrase

5 🔘 *2.09* Allow a minute for the class to look at the Quick steps and the Exam tip, and take any questions. Then play the recording through, without pausing. Allow a minute at the end for them to check they have answered all the questions and spelt everything correctly, then go through the answers. Also ask them whether their answers in Exercise 3 were accurate or not.

If you wish, photocopy the script on page 80 for your students and ask them to underline the sections which give the answers.

Exam task

> **Answers**
>
> **1** eyesight   **2** reserve   **3** flight engineer   **4** 12 / twelve hours
> **5** views (you get)   **6** criticism   **7** 3,000 / three thousand
> **8** the economic situation / the economy

> **Recording script**
>
> *You'll hear airline pilot Anita Ricci talking about her work. For questions 1–8, complete the sentences with a word or short phrase. You now have 45 seconds to look at Part 2.*
>
> It's a fabulous job to have, though when I was turned down by the Air Force I thought I'd never actually be a pilot. I had the right degree, I performed well in the psychological test and my general fitness level was fine, but (1) it was my eyesight that let me down. It just didn't meet the standards required for flying combat aircraft. Fortunately, though, I was accepted for training at a civilian flying school.
>
> To become a pilot there's a huge amount to learn, from physics and meteorology to navigation and understanding aircraft systems. And even when you qualify it's highly unlikely your first job will be as a regular pilot. (2) You'll probably be a reserve pilot, waiting on call at or near an airport rather like passengers on standby – except that you'll have to be on the plane within 90 minutes to help fly it.
>
> There are normally two pilots on the flight deck: the captain and the first officer. (3) Some older aircraft might also have a flight engineer, though as happened with radio operators and navigators several decades ago they're being replaced by technology, in this case by computers.

The working hours aren't bad, with around 14 days a month off. Though for someone like me who's (4) <u>currently flying between Europe and South America</u>, some of those are inevitably spent far from home. <u>For international flights</u> you can be on duty up to sixteen hours, of which <u>twelve are the most you can spend continuously at the controls</u>, whereas for domestic routes the maximum is eight hours without a break.

Naturally, you particularly enjoy landing in certain places. Some because you're arriving in warm sunny weather in the southern hemisphere when it's gloomy midwinter in the north, while (5) <u>at others it's the great views you get from the flight deck window, especially in Switzerland, say</u>.

For some pilots the downside is the testing that takes place twice a year, throughout your career. And if you're not up to scratch, you're out of a job. It's as simple as that and I don't have a problem with it. I know that as in any profession there's always room for improvement, so (6) <u>whenever I receive criticism I try to learn from it, knowing that what is said is always meant constructively</u>.

In many ways I'm fortunate to have this job. Few pilots are taken on by major airlines and fewer still reach senior positions where they may earn a hundred thousand a year. (7) <u>Not long ago this airline had three thousand applications when they advertised twenty-five posts. They were all from qualified pilots.</u>

And even if you are taken on, job security is not great. Major airlines have been known to go out of business, and (8) <u>any ups or downs in the economic situation tend to have a disproportionate effect on the airline industry</u>. Routes may be cut and aircraft orders cancelled. So if you're thinking of a career as a pilot, choose your airline carefully – then stick with it.

See the Workbook for further practice.

Speaking

Adding emphasis

1 Explain that these emphatic forms, sometimes called *introductory 'what'* or *introductory 'it'*, are used in both spoken and written English, and can be extended to other expressions such as *all, the thing (that), the place (where)*. Also remind the class that *what* means *the thing that*, and therefore is not a relative pronoun. Give pairs a few minutes to study and answer these, then go through the answers, eliciting more examples with each expression, using different tenses.

> **Answers**
>
> **a)** is   **b)** was   **c)** was   **d)** was
> **a)** 1 physics   2 What   3 the background information   4 no
> **b)** 1 I needed the money   2 The reason   3 the background information   4 that
> **c)** 1 the manager   2 The person   3 the background information   4 who
> **d)** 1 last month   2 It   3 It   4 when

2 Allow two or three minutes for pairs to note down their answers, then check.

> **Answers**
>
> 1 What you need to do is work harder.
> 2 It is travelling to work that causes the most stress.
> 3 The people who seem to make the most money are bankers.
> 4 The reason Emma resigned was that she didn't like her boss.
> 5 It was all the form-filling that I found really boring.
> 6 The place where my friend and I first met was the office.

3 Encourage pairs to use a range of different expressions from Exercises 1 and 2, and where possible to make follow-up comments or ask questions using these forms, e.g. 1 *It's science that has always interested me.* Elicit some answers when they have finished.

> **Suggested answers**
>
> 1 What I'd most like to do is be an astronomer.
> 2 What I find really boring is tidying my room.
> 3 The country where I'd most like to live is Australia.
> 4 The people who annoy me most are those who keep trying to sell you things over the phone.
> 5 It's in August that I feel most relaxed.
> 6 What I most want to achieve is happiness at work and at home.

Part 4

4 🔘 *2.10* Refer students to the Quick steps. Point out to the class that they will hear the teacher ask one question and the students' replies. Play the recording through without pausing, then check the answers.

> **Answers**
>
> 1 Do you think people should choose a career when they are very young?
> 2 Maxim
> 3 No, only partly.

5 🔘 *2.10* Play the recording again, pausing if necessary. Then check their answers, and elicit others the class may know for 1 and 2, e.g. *I'd go along with most of that, but ...; That's a difficult one. On the one hand ...* . If you wish, photocopy the recording script on page 81 for the students to check their answers.

> **Answers**
>
> 1 It's hard to say.   2 To a certain extent, yes, but ... You could argue that ...   3 what matters is; it's the young people who ...

> **Recording script**
>
> Teacher: Maxim, do you think people should choose a career when they are very young?
>
> Maxim: I'm sorry, could you repeat that?
>
> Teacher: Do you think people should choose a career when they are very young?

Maxim:	It's hard to say. You could argue that the people who do best in life are the ones who decide at an early age what they want to do and then get on and work towards that. But given that most people will probably have more than one career as society changes and technology develops, some would say there's no real hurry. So maybe what matters is being able to acquire skills when they become necessary, rather than trying to make plans now for an uncertain future.
Teacher:	Do you agree, Dariya?
Dariya:	To a certain extent, yes, but I do think it's the young people who already know they want to be doctors, lawyers, teachers and so on who will ultimately be the most successful, particularly as they'll be in professions that will always be needed. And I don't think they'll ever be replaced by computers, either.

6 Refer students to the Speaking guide on page 111. Tell the class to play the roles of 'examiner' and 'candidates'. Remind the candidates that they can ask for repetition of the questions, but the examiners cannot rephrase or add to the printed questions apart from adding the prompts given in the bullet points. Encourage the use of emphatic forms from Exercises 1–3. Groups could begin simultaneously so that you can ensure that each Part 4 lasts about five minutes. Remind groups to be polite and constructive in their comments. Finish with a class round-up, asking what difficulties were encountered and making a note of these for future classwork. Refer students to the point in the Exam tip.

Writing

Formal language

1 Check that all the terms used are clear, giving or eliciting examples if necessary, then give pairs a minute or two to do this. Go through the answers, reminding the class that there may be exceptions, especially in more neutral styles of writing, and particularly in emails.

> **Answers**
>
> formal 1, 3, 4, 8   informal 2, 5, 6, 7, 9, 10

2 Some of these informal expressions may be new to the class, but tell them they are often used in everyday speech and the meanings here should be clear from the context. Give pairs a couple of minutes to do the exercise, then check their answers and elicit more examples of both the formal and the informal expressions.

> **Answers**
>
> 1 I am quite interested in   2 excessive   3 misunderstand me   4 fortunate   5 I was completely unaware   6 extremely disappointed   7 understand the situation   8 are well informed

> See the Workbook for further practice.

Part 2: formal letter

3 Ask the class if many students in their country/ies go on work experience, and if so what it usually consists of. Give groups plenty of time to discuss these points, if necessary feeding in prompts from *Suggested answers*. Do a round-up when everyone has finished, encouraging groups to exchange ideas and also possibly practical advice on obtaining work experience placements.

> **Suggested answers**
>
> 1 It looks good on the CV, making it easier for students to find permanent work when they leave school/college. It shows future employers you have motivation and interest in that field. It introduces a teenager to the world of work. It can give a young person ideas for a future career. It can identify skills, and weaknesses, that they may not have known they have. They can try out different kinds of work without any commitment. They get the chance to speak to employees to find out what working in that industry is really like. They can make contacts in that industry. They might even find their work becomes permanent.
> 2 Raising the company's profile within the local community. Helping young people who are entering the labour market adapt more easily to work and a working environment. Developing recruitment channels. Raising awareness of career opportunities within the company.
> 3 Students' own answers.

4 Allow 30 seconds for the class to look at the exam task, then go through the answers. Suggest they ask themselves questions like these whenever they are about to do a letter-writing task.

> **Answers**
>
> 1 a local college   2 To tell the college that your company has vacancies for students who wish to do two weeks' work experience during the next summer term.   3 Information about what your company does, the kind of work the students would do, and how they would benefit from working there.   4 formal

5 Pairs should be able to do this in two minutes. Go through the answers, pointing out that they may find some of the 'appropriate' expressions useful when they write their own letter.

> **Answers**
>
> 1 inappropriate: *chill out* and *mates* are too informal
> 2 appropriate   3 inappropriate: *we've got, loads, fun* (adjective) and *guys* are too informal   4 appropriate   5 inappropriate: *check out, info* and the exclamation mark are too informal
> 6 appropriate   7 appropriate   8 inappropriate: it is an email or text message ending

6 Allow pairs about three minutes to gist read the letter and identify the paragraph which contains each of 1–6. Check their answers.

> **Answers**
>
> 1 3rd paragraph   2 2nd paragraph   3 1st paragraph
> 4 last paragraph/line   5 1st paragraph   6 4th paragraph

7 Give pairs plenty of time to answer these questions. Go through the answers, eliciting more features of formal language such as long, sometimes complex, sentences; formal linking expressions such as *in addition* and *moreover*; passive verb forms. Point out that *CV* is one of those abbreviations (like *BBC*) that is acceptable in formal writing.

> **Answers**
>
> **1** fairly formal   **2** Dear Sir or Madam; Yours faithfully,
> **3** the majority of whom; both of which
> **4** What will benefit them most, however, is ...
> **5** tell – inform, big – extensive, gym – gymnasium, staff – employees, training – instruction, begins – commences, looking for – seeking, very pleased – most grateful

8 Give the class a minute to study the exam task, then elicit the answers. Make sure everyone understands that they must cover three main points in their letter.

> **Answers**
>
> **1** Ms Klaudia Nowak, Human Resources Manager, Central Hotel   **2** To apply for work experience   **3** Details of the kind of hotel work you would like to do and why, the reasons why you would be suited to working in a hotel environment, what you hope to learn from the experience.   **4** formal

9 Elicit the answers and tell the class they can use some of the relevant points as prompts. Students then work on their own, noting down points to include and putting them under suitable paragraph headings based on three points they identified in Exercise 8. Allow at least five minutes for this.

> **Answers**
>
> Relevant – 1, 3, 5, 7, 8

10 Refer students to the Writing guide, page 101, before they begin and remind them about the point in the Exam tip. Give the class 35 minutes for the writing, as they have already studied the task and planned their letter. Remind them to leave plenty of time at the end for checking.

For further speaking practice, pairs could swap letters and then interview each other for the jobs they've applied for.

Model answer

Dear Ms Nowak,

I am writing to apply to do work experience at the Central Hotel this summer, as advertised in today's newspaper. I am aged seventeen and next year will be my final year at school, after which I hope to attend college to study to become a chef.

I would therefore be most interested in working in the hotel kitchens, if possible as a chef's assistant. I already have some experience of this kind of work, having recently helped my uncle and aunt prepare meals at their restaurant during the school holidays.

I have always had a keen interest in food and cooking, taking great satisfaction from preparing healthy and appetising meals. I also enjoy working as part of a team. This, I am sure, is extremely important in the kitchens of such a large hotel where so many different kinds of food need to be prepared. In addition, I am capable of working under pressure, for example when there is a sudden rush of orders and very little time in which to prepare the meals.

Working alongside expert chefs would teach me an enormous amount about cooking and food presentation. As well as learning new techniques, I would discover how to prepare new dishes and also how to improve those I already make. Above all, I would be in an environment where my creative skills could develop, simply by observing professionals in action and, I hope, talking to them about their work.

I enclose my CV and look forward to hearing from you.

Yours sincerely,
Jaime Alonso

See the Workbook and CD-ROM for further practice.

9

Science and technology

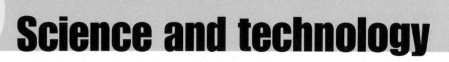

Unit objectives

TOPICS	science & technology
GRAMMAR	modals, including continuous & passive forms
VOCABULARY	dependent prepositions; science lexis
READING AND USE OF ENGLISH	Part 2: open cloze; Part 5: multiple-choice questions
WRITING	Part 2 report: result links, text organisation
LISTENING	Part 3: long text, multiple-choice questions
SPEAKING	Part 2: speculating about present & past

Listening

Science vocabulary

1 Explain that these words are some of the most common in the academic language of science, but all are also used in non-scientific contexts. Allow the use of dictionaries, and take questions where necessary. Tell groups to give reasons when discussing each of the points, then allow about five minutes for them to do so. Do a quick round-up of their opinions when they have finished.

> See the CD-ROM for further practice.

Part 3

2 Students stay in their groups to discuss these points, which relate to the content of the exam task recording.

> **Suggested answers**
>
> 1 Groups of students from different schools or colleges present scientific projects in the hope of winning a prize for the best in different categories, usually based on age. A panel of judges studies each project, and the students are interviewed about it. Preparation usually takes months once a group has chosen the topic for their project, usually involving both classwork and homework.

Exam task

🔘 *2.11* Before doing the Exam task, focus attention on the Quick steps and Exam tip.

If you wish, photocopy the script on page 82 for your students and ask them to underline the sections which give the answers.

> **Answers**
>
> **1** B **2** A **3** A **4** B **5** D **6** B

> **Recording script**
>
> *You'll hear an interview with Physics teacher Kieran Shaw, who has taken his students to a Science Fair. For questions 1–6, choose the best answer (A, B, C or D) which fits best according to what you hear. You now have 70 seconds to look at Part 3.*

Interviewer: Good morning from the conference centre, where the Science Fair is taking place. It's an annual event designed to give young people the opportunity to learn more about the scientific process through experimentation, problem solving, and in-depth learning. With me is Kieran Shaw, a Physics teacher accompanying his students. Tell me, Kieran, what do you think of this fair compared to that of previous years?

Kieran: It's excellent, certainly up to last year's already high standards as far as the projects themselves are concerned, and with the same number entered, which I think is about right. I just hope they manage to avoid (1) <u>last year's row over the final choice of winners, which was controversial to say the least</u>. There's a different panel this time and that should make a difference, but there's no change in their policy of awarding three prizes in each category, and I think that also makes sense.

Interviewer: You say the numbers taking part here have held up, but is that the case in other fairs?

Kieran: Not everywhere, no. And I'm a little worried that we might start to see fewer people taking part in them generally.

Interviewer: Is that because of the economic situation, with schools having to make cutbacks?

Kieran: In most cases it costs schools little or nothing for students to attend, so that's unlikely to be a factor, and neither is the expense involved in developing and presenting the projects, which most students' families find reasonably affordable. (2) <u>Of more concern is the feeling in some quarters that actually going somewhere to see science in action belongs to the pre-internet era,</u> though the majority of the students themselves seem as keen as ever to attend fairs, despite the fact that it usually means giving up a Saturday to do so!

Interviewer: There are also some issues surrounding the fairs themselves, aren't there?

Kieran: Yes, one of the key ones being the traditional male dominance of science subjects, leading to girls being under-represented in these projects – though happily there's a good gender balance across my groups. They're also good at working in and between groups, so there isn't the over-competitive atmosphere that some people complain about. (3) <u>A more valid point is that someone whose father, say, is a chemist may not be doing all the work themselves, and I have had to look into one or two cases like that.</u> It's also sometimes alleged that those from wealthy backgrounds can afford to go for more complex projects, but I think there's a good socio-economic mix in each of my groups, too.

Interviewer: So what's the main criterion when selecting a topic? Its originality?

Kieran:	Well, that's certainly a factor to take into account, but (4) <u>first and foremost it must be something capable of holding the participants' attention over the months leading up to the fair.</u> Avoiding areas that might be too complicated for young students to explain clearly in their presentation matters, too – as, by the way, does anything that may require spending a lot on apparatus – but not to the same extent.
Interviewer:	How do students get on doing their presentations? I imagine some are pretty nervous.
Kieran:	Yes, and to overcome their nerves some of them try to learn everything off by heart and then make a speech to the judges, which of course isn't how it works. The judges will look at the display and perhaps briefly at their notes, and then ask them some questions. It's important they don't rush their answers, but it's also best to keep them simple, (5) <u>avoiding any jargon they're unable to explain if asked to by the judges. That happens quite often, and doesn't give a good impression.</u> The important thing is knowing what everything in their notes means, and being able to answer questions about it.
Interviewer:	Finally, Kieran, which project do you think will win in the senior category?
Kieran:	I'd say there are three clear front runners, and (6) <u>the odds are that the one measuring the amount of bacteria present on various kitchen utensils will come out on top.</u> Of course, I'd rather the project on where fresh cherries deteriorate most slowly won because that's my group's entry, but I don't think it'll happen for them this time. As runner-up, I'd pick the one about whether the quality of our vision is different in the morning and afternoon. Or perhaps the one designed to test the theory that it is best to wear black in hot weather because it's much more efficient than white at absorbing heat from our body – which of course is a much closer energy source than the sun.
Interviewer:	You learn something every day! Thank you, Kieran.

For extra speaking practice, tell students to imagine they are planning a science project. Ask them to work in pairs or small groups and suggest how they would test the following ideas. They can use expressions from Exercise 1. They don't need to plan complete projects but just note down some ideas for each. Elicit some answers from the different groups.

1 Why some plants grow better indoors than outside the house.

2 The kind of insulation that best prevents heat loss.

3 Whether there is a relationship between people's ages and their reaction times.

4 Which design of road bridge is the strongest.

5 Whether some colours are brighter when shining through fog than others.

6 How effective different types of soap are at removing bacteria from hands.

Suggested answers

1 Different kinds of plant growing both indoors and outdoors: check variables such as amount and intensity of direct sunlight, evaporation levels, temperature variations, wind, insects, etc.
2 Heat water in a container: measure speed of fall in temperature when container is wrapped in a variety of insulating materials.
3 People of different age groups: test their reaction times to different kinds of stimulus by touching a screen or clicking a mouse.
4 Make models of each using a 3D printer: test using weights at different points of the road surface, and test total load capacity.
5 Create fog-like conditions in a large container. Shine different coloured lights through it, starting at low intensity. Measure which become visible first, but check whether everyone has the same perception or not.
6 Fill a dish with a coloured liquid that highlights bacteria on skin. Wash hands after contact with a range of (preferably unpleasant!) materials using different kinds of soap, place hands in liquid and then photograph them.

See the Workbook and CD-ROM for further practice.

Grammar

Modal verbs

1 Give pairs a couple of minutes to complete the exercise. Point out that there may be more than one possible answer in some cases. Go through the answers, eliciting the reason in each case. Refer students to the Grammar reference on page 96 if necessary.

Answers

1 could → was able to: for a specific occasion in the past.
2 must → had to: *had to* is the past form of *must*.
3 can → might / may: for a specific possibility.
4 mustn't → don't need to / needn't / don't have to: *mustn't* is for a prohibition.
5 can → might / may / could have: the form *can have + -ed* is never used.
6 had to be → must have been: a deduction about the past. *Had to* is for an obligation in the past.
7 can be → could have been prevented: past theoretical possibility. *Can be* is the present form.
8 needn't → didn't need to: it wasn't necessary to do it. *Needn't* is the present form.

2 Allow five minutes for pairs to note down their answers, then check. Elicit more examples with the correct and incorrect forms.

Answers

1 can: possibility   2 shouldn't: criticism of past action
3 could: theoretical past possibility   4 must: deduction
5 needn't: no necessity   6 might: past possibility   7 can't: deduction about the past   8 must: deduction about the past   9 should: advice   10 needn't have taken: action done unnecessarily

3 This could be done either as a written exercise or verbally in pairs, with one student making each comment and the other replying. Point out that more than one answer will be possible in each case, e.g. *I suppose you could have seen me there, yes.* Check their answers and elicit variations from those given below.

> ### Suggested answers
>
> **1** There must be thousands.   **2** You shouldn't have spent so much, then.   **3** Oh, we didn't have to do double maths at my school.   **4** It must have been stolen, I'm afraid.   **5** They might have been held up by traffic.   **6** Yes, I wasn't able to answer many questions, either.   **7** He needn't have taken it there!   **8** You can't have done. Everyone knows aliens don't exist.

4 Explain that modal forms are sometimes tested in Reading and Use of English Part 4, and that these are examples of that type of item. Tell the class to do these on their own in about 12 minutes, then check their answers.

Exam task

> ### Answers
>
> **1** I should have / should've | sent her   **2** I could | have / could've completed   **3** did not / didn't have | to make   **4** might have | accidentally broken   **5** should not / shouldn't have | been allowed to   **6** must have / must've forgotten | that she said

See the Workbook for further practice.

Reading and Use of English

Part 5

1 Point out that question 2 is particularly relevant to the topic of the reading text. Pairs discuss questions 1 and 2 for three or four minutes. Elicit some of the answers.

2 Tell the class to do this gist-reading activity on their own. Allow two or three minutes, then elicit the answers to questions 1 & 2.

> ### Answers
>
> **1** a) stupid   b) lowering the level of difficulty and the intellectual content
> **2** The writer wants to see an improvement in science broadcasting.

3 Allow a minute for the class to look at the question stems, then elicit the answers. Remind them to check the focus of each question whenever they do Reading and Use of English Part 5.

> ### Answers
>
> **a)** 2, 3, 4   **b)** 6   **c)** 5   **d)** 1

4 Give the class 15 minutes to do the exam task, working on their own. Go through the answers but leave any vocabulary questions until after they have done Exercise 5.

> ### Answers
>
> **1** B   **2** A   **3** C   **4** D   **5** D   **6** B

5 Give pairs a couple of minutes to find these. Then go through the answers, eliciting more examples using some or all of them. Point out the formal usage of *the former*, and elicit the phrase used for the second of two things: *the latter*. Also focus on the Latin origin of the formal phrase *the status quo*, and ask whether it is also used in their first language(s).

> ### Answers
>
> **1** Cue   **2** take a dim view   **3** the former   **4** in a sense   **5** is a matter of   **6** in play   **7** the odd   **8** the status quo

See the Workbook and CD-ROM for further practice.

Part 2

Dependent prepositions

1 Make it clear that this heading does not cover the *to* which follows adjectives in expressions followed directly by verbs, e.g. *due to, inclined to, bound to*, where it forms part of the infinitive. Also point out that although these are the most common collocations, students may see others such as *restricted by* or *superior in*, or some of these adjectives with other prepositions, e.g. *biased towards*. Give pairs four or five minutes to note down the phrases they form, then go through the answers, eliciting an example sentence with each.

> ### Answers
>
> alert to, biased against, compatible with, deprived of, eligible for, equivalent to, frustrated by, hostile to, inadequate for, insensitive to, knowledgeable about, notorious for, prejudiced against, protective of, resident in, restricted to, superior to, untouched by

2 Tell the class they can use dictionaries if necessary for some of these adjectives, checking the likely prepositions as they do so. Allow four or five minutes for this, then go through the answers, eliciting more example sentences with each collocation.

> ### Answers
>
> **1** adjacent to   **2** correct   **3** handy for   **4** correct   **5** receptive to   **6** correct   **7** horrified by   **8** sceptical about

3 Students have already seen all these collocations, but they now need to focus on the meanings in context. Give pairs about two minutes to note down their answers, then check.

> ### Answers
>
> **1** restricted to   **2** handy for   **3** equivalent to   **4** sceptical about   **5** eligible for   **6** ignorant of   **7** notorious for   **8** renowned for

See the CD-ROM for further practice.

4 Give the class a minute or two to gist read, then elicit answers.

> **Suggested answers**
>
> Because we can only hear one side of the dialogue, we have to concentrate particularly hard to try to understand what it is about.

5 Refer students to the Quick steps. Give the class, working individually, ten minutes to do the exam task. After they have finished, focusing particularly on the collocations formed by dependent prepositions.

Exam task

> **Answers**
>
> **1** according   **2** for / to   **3** takes / took   **4** to   **5** of   **6** who
> **7** by   **8** Not

Speaking

Speculating

1 🔘 2.12 Tell the class they need to use one, two or three words in each gap, and that more than one answer may be possible. Give pairs a minute to do this, then play the recording once, which should be enough. Go through the answers, asking about other words they used. Point out that all these forms are very useful for talking about what is possibly happening in Speaking Part 2 pictures.

> **Answers**
>
> (Contracted forms also possible) **1** must have been
> **2** must have   **3** might / could / may / must be   **4** might / could / may
> **5** might / could / may be

> **Recording script**
>
> A: Hey, that's a long queue!
>
> B: Some of them are looking fed up. They must've been standing there for hours.
>
> A: Yes, they must've been. I wonder why?
>
> B: They might be hoping to get tickets for that concert.
>
> A: I suppose they might be. Or they may be queuing for the sales. They start later today.

2 Tell the class they can use either the present or the perfect form of the modals *might, may, could* or *must* plus *-ing*. Give pairs a few minutes to do these, monitoring for accuracy, then elicit some answers.

> **Suggested answers**
>
> **1** He might / could / may / must have been revising all night.
> **2** They could / may / might be winning 4–0.
> **3** They must be going through a tunnel.
> **4** It must have been snowing all night.
> **5** She could / may / might be out shopping. / She might have gone shopping.
> **6** I must have been dreaming.

Part 2

3 🔘 2.13 Point out that both students are strong Advanced students. Play the recording once without pausing, then ask the class for their answers.

> **Answers**
>
> **1** the office workers and the farmer   **2** by hand in both cases   **3** farmer: learning to use the machinery, having to concentrate   office workers: having to concentrate on a screen, tiring, risk to eyesight, email interruptions   **4** The robot in the operating theatre. She thinks this has been most beneficial to society as it can help cure people more easily and avoids mistakes that even good surgeons can make.

> **Recording script**
>
> Teacher: Nico, it's your turn first. Here are your pictures. They show people working with different kinds of technology. Compare two of the pictures, and say how the jobs might have been done in the past, and how difficult it might be for the people to work with this technology.
>
> Nico: They show people doing jobs using computers and modern machinery. Although the first photo shows people indoors and the other is outside in the fields, it must be a lot easier for them now than before that technology was invented.
>
> The people indoors <u>may be</u> <u>preparing</u> to give a presentation. They <u>might be researching</u> facts and figures online which previously <u>must have been</u> very difficult to find. The massive machine <u>might be harvesting</u> crops and the farmer <u>could be</u> <u>using</u> the computer to check the machine is working properly. It probably takes a day to harvest a field now whereas in olden times it <u>must have taken</u> many days to do by hand.
>
> It <u>must have been</u> back-breaking work, too, so it's made life much easier for farmers. Learning to use that machinery, though, <u>might not have been</u> so easy for people used to working entirely with their hands. So they have to concentrate hard, which they didn't really need to do in the past. The office workers, too, <u>must be concentrating</u> hard on the screen, and if they do that all day it could get very tiring, especially for their eyes. They <u>might also be getting interrupted</u> all the time by emails, which didn't use to happen back in the days when everything was done on paper!
>
> Teacher: Mia, which of these technological advances do you think is the most beneficial to society?
>
> Mia: Probably the robot, er, in the operating theatre. With all the progress in microsurgery that's making it possible to cure illnesses and injuries more easily, these devices <u>must be saving</u> many lives. And by replacing humans, they avoid the risk of mistakes that even the most skilled surgeons can sometimes make. Also, some robots enable operations to be carried out in remote parts of the world where there aren't many doctors.
>
> Teacher: Thank you.

4 ◯ `2.13` Play the recording once or twice more, as necessary, then go through the answers underlined in the recording script above.

> ### Answers
> modal + *be* + *-ing*: may be doing, might be using, might be feeling, must be concentrating, might (also) be getting interrupted, must be saving
> modal + *have* + pp: must (surely) have taken, must have been, might not have been

5 Monitor groups, ensuring that all As and Bs speak for about the right length of time, and there are no interruptions before time is up.

6 Remind groups to be honest and constructive in their comments. When they have all finished, ask the class for the general impressions but not for comments on individual students. Students can check the Speaking guide, page 108, for homework.

Writing

Result links

1 Give pairs a couple of minutes to fill in the gaps, which they should be able to do without using dictionaries. Go through the answers, eliciting more example sentences if time allows.

> ### Answers
> **1** reason – for that reason   **2** so – so...that   **3** owing – owing to   **4** Otherwise   **5** consequence – in consequence   **6** account – on account of   **7** such – such a...that   **8** else – or else   **9** Consequently   **10** view – in view of (the fact that)
> *Formal phrases*: owing to, on account of, consequently, in view of the fact that

2 Point out there may be various ways of rewriting these, but tell students – working on their own – just to write one sentence for each. Allow about five minutes, then check their work.

> ### Suggested answers
> **1** The project had gone over budget and in consequence, it was abandoned.
> **2** The instructions were so complicated that I couldn't understand them.
> **3** On account of a defect, the device was withdrawn from sale.
> **4** You'd better charge up your phone up soon, or else the battery will run out.
> **5** A virus got into the system. Consequently, all the computers crashed.
> **6** That's such an addictive game that I can't stop playing it.
> **7** Owing to the sudden rise in temperature, the machine stopped working.
> **8** I don't keep looking at my email. Otherwise, I'd spend all day answering messages.

> See the Workbook for further practice.

Part 2: report

3 Let pairs discuss the questions for a few minutes, using result links wherever possible. Then do a brief round-up of answers.

> ### Suggested answers
> **1** Working with state-of-the-art technology, the possibility of making new discoveries.
> **2** Archaelogist discovering ancient civilizations, biochemist discovering a cure for a disease.
> **3** Students' own answers.

4 Give the class half a minute to study the exam task, then elicit the answers. Remind them to ask themselves questions like these whenever they begin a Part 2 report task. Refer students to page 103 of the Writing guide.

> ### Answers
> **1** Attitudes towards science among students at your school.
> **2** The head teacher; they want to increase the proportion of its students studying science subjects to advanced level.
> **3** An evaluation of the appeal of science at the school; an explanation of why comparatively few students say they want to become scientists; suggestions for ways of encouraging more of them to consider a future career in science.

5 Allow about three minutes for individuals to gist read the text and label the paragraphs. Elicit some of their suggestions, pointing out that there are many possible headings, especially for paragraphs B and C.

> ### Suggested answers
> **A** Introduction   **B** Viewing science lessons positively
> **C** Viewing science lessons negatively   **D** The media view
> **E** Suggestions

6 Give pairs plenty of time to go through the text and discuss question 5, then elicit the answers.

> ### Answers
> **1** An evaluation of the appeal of science at the school: B & C
> An explanation of why comparatively few students want to become scientists: D
> Suggestions for ways of encouraging more of them to consider a future career in science: E
> **2** *This report focuses on ...*
> **3** Fairly formal, e.g. complete sentences; no contracted forms; formal linkers such as *moreover* and *in addition*; long words, e.g. *stimulating environment*; full forms of words, e.g. *laboratory*; less common words, e.g. *perceived*; formal structures, e.g. *the suspicion with which*, passive forms, e.g. *concern has been expressed*; impersonal structures such as *there is a widespread belief that*
> **4** B: *in consequence*   C: *owing to*
> **5** Students should be invited to participate in Science Fair projects, scientific work experience programmes and virtual Open Days at university science faculties; they should be made aware of the benefits of studying science.

7 Let the class look quickly at the task, then elicit the answers. Check they understand what they have to do.

> **Answers**
> **1** An electronic device you always take with you when you travel on business.
> **2** Colleagues, they are about to begin making similar trips themselves.
> **3** An explanation of why you chose that kind of device, an evaluation of its usefulness in practice, suggestions for how it could be improved.

8 Allow a few minutes for this brainstorming activity, but don't elicit answers.

9 Tell the class to work on their own, first noting down points to include and then putting those under headings, if they choose to use them, or under paragraph numbers. Allow five minutes for this, then tell them to go on to the actual writing in Exercise 10.

10 Give the class 35–40 minutes to write their reports, as they have already studied the task and planned their text. Remind them to leave a few minutes at the end for checking.

> **Model answer**
>
> ### An essential travel item
>
> Introduction
> The purpose of this report is to provide information on a device that is particularly useful when travelling. That, without doubt, is a tablet, a mobile computer produced by various manufacturers.
>
> Reasons for choosing a tablet
> The frequent business traveller requires a terminal which can be operated by means of both a touchscreen and keyboard, has substantial memory for storing data, and is sufficiently compact and lightweight to enable easy transportation. Tablets are the only device that currently meet all these criteria, as laptops are excessively bulky and mobile phones lack a full-size keyboard.
>
> Advantages of a tablet
> Despite its size, a higher-specification model has many of the capabilities of a desktop PC. In consequence, it can be used for work purposes virtually anywhere. Most tablets have built-in wi-fi, fit easily into hand luggage, and are ideal for reading documents and journals, viewing diagrams and photographs, or sending and receiving emails.
>
> Disadvantages of a tablet
> Criticisms of the tablet include the shape of the screen, which is not ideally suited to watching videos, the lack of USB ports to connect with other appliances, and the difficulty some experience in using the virtual keyboard, especially when keying in longer documents. Another frequent complaint is that the battery tends to run out alarmingly quickly.
>
> Recommendations
> New models could incorporate features designed to deal with these issues, although keeping the device small must surely remain a priority. However, the manufacturers could consider installing more applications. These might, for instance, enable wireless printing, or background music while you work.

> See the Workbook for further practice.

10

A mind of one's own

Unit objectives

TOPICS	psychology & personality
GRAMMAR	wishes & regrets
VOCABULARY	three-part phrasal verbs; adjectives of personality
READING AND USE OF ENGLISH	Part 4: key word transformations; Part 6: cross-text multiple matching
WRITING	Part 1: concession, opening paragraphs
LISTENING	Part 4: multiple matching
SPEAKING	Parts 3 & 4: negotiating, reaching a decision

Reading and Use of English

Part 6

1 Make sure the class understand the word *trait*. Tell them to use the prefixes as clues, then discuss the pictures in pairs. Elicit the answers and move on to the quiz that relates to this in Exercise 2.

Answers

1 a) extrovert b) introvert
2 A: introvert B: extrovert
3 The extrovert may be happier, louder, and possibly more annoying! The introvert may prefer working on their own, writing rather than talking, and find it more difficult to make friends.

2 Tell the class this is a light-hearted quiz they can do on their own, and that they won't have to tell anyone their scores if they don't want to. Give them about three minutes to answer, then explain their results (below) to them. Go through each question without asking which answer individuals chose, asking the class which indicates extroversion and which introversion.

Answers

Each *yes* scores 1 point. The closer to a total of 12, the more introvert people probably are; the closer to a total of 0, they more extrovert they are likely to be. The nearer to 6 their score is, the nearer to being an *ambivert* they are. But point out that even if someone answered every single question as an introvert or extrovert, that doesn't mean that their behaviour is predictable in all circumstances.

3 Tell pairs they can use dictionaries for these words, all of which appear in the exam text. Go through the answers when they have finished.

Answers

1 classification   2 proposition   3 consistently   4 questionable
5 merit   6 perception

4 Give the class two or three minutes to do this gist-reading activity on their own, then check their answers.

Answers

generally positive: D
generally negative: A, B
partly positive and partly negative: C

5 Allow a minute for this, then check.

Suggested answers

1 1 similar criticism, lack of objectivity, B
  2 disagrees, C, main argument
  3 different, others, two categories
  4 different, D, who, enjoy
2 item 3

6 Refer students to the Quick steps and the Exam tip. Give the class fifteen minutes to do this, working on their own. Go through the answers but leave any vocabulary questions until after they have done Exercise 6. To help, the text is included below with the answers underlined. These are the sections the students should have marked.

Answers

1 C   2 A   3 D   4 A

Quiet

Four reviewers comment on Susan Cain's book Quiet: The Power of Introverts in a World That Can't Stop Talking

A Cain's central proposition is that over the past century the US has moved from a 'culture of character' to a 'culture of personality', as social admiration has shifted from ideals of private honour to public perception, leading to the inexorable rise of the 'extrovert ideal'. (2) I find this highly questionable, and Cain also appears to be setting up (3) a new categorisation which does not hold water. Extrovert and introvert are simply not the same sort of things as female/male, black/white or alive/dead; it is more useful to see the terms as adjectives, describing points on a long, loose arc than as identities. Overall, this is a remarkably noisy 'extroverted' book, bombarding the reader with unharmonious 'facts' and psychobabble ('over stimulating', to use one of Cain's terms). (4) Lovers of quiet won't like Quiet – we would rather go for a nice walk in the country.

B *Quiet* is written for introverts. (1) This involves telling us how great introverts are, how they are so sensitive you can measure their responses to things by how much their pupils dilate when faced with loud music or flashing lights. They think harder about things before they do them, and spend fruitful hours alone. At some points in this book, it is hard to avoid the impression that extroverts are bullies or at least that (3) Cain's simplistic extrovert/introvert contrast is really a balance of jock versus geek, played out so reliably in movies about US high schools. Cain does everything she can to play this down, and say that extroverts can read this book, too (she has sales to consider, after all); but in test after test, outgoing individuals respond less well to difficult upbringings, cope less well when deprived of sleep, and are missing out on the evolutionary advantages of blushing.

C This book has a simple, convincing idea at its heart: that the western world has become so enamoured of what Susan Cain calls the 'extrovert ideal' that it is missing out on the talents of half its population. If you can't speak in public, wilt in meetings and hate networking, then you are an introvert and you are destined to be ignored by an attention-deficit world. (2) <u>Cain argues – correctly, I think – that this is mad. It is a strong point and she brings in serious data to back it up.</u> In the end, though, (3) <u>her insistence that one of two sizes fits all means that this book becomes little more than another</u> <u>*Men Are From Mars, Women Are From Venus*</u> <u>tick-box work.</u> People are more complicated, subtle and surprising than these either-or classifications. And (1) <u>not every introvert is an unrecognised genius, nor every extrovert an idiot thug.</u>

D Recognising the complexity of human nature, the author of *Quiet* avoids falling into the trap of labelling introversion and extroversion as a clearly-defined distinction. (3) <u>Instead, Susan Cain's approach is to treat them as two extremes on a scale that covers a whole range of personality types, each with its own particular characteristics.</u> Unlike others who have published works on this topic, she makes no judgment on the relative merits of tending towards one of these extremes or the other, and in fact calls for greater objectivity when assessing the weaker and stronger points of extroverts and introverts. (4) <u>That in itself is one reason why this perceptive and consistently readable book is particularly likely to appeal to those who regard themselves as belonging to the latter group.</u>

7 Give pairs two or three minutes to work through these, then elicit answers. Point out that *miss out on* and *stand up for* are examples of a 3-part phrasal verbs, which are covered in Use of English in this unit.

> **Answers**
>
> **1** establish   **2** show happening or developing   **3** minimise the importance of   **4** fail to get an advantage from   **5** support   **6** demand that something should happen

8 Working individually or in pairs, students complete the sentences. Remind them they need to think about whether the form needs to change or not. Point out that the number of spaces indicates the number of words required. Check answers and possibly elicit more example sentences.

> **Answers**
>
> **1** play down   **2** played out   **3** backed up   **4** set up   **5** called for   **6** miss out on

> See the Workbook and CD-ROM for further practice.

Grammar

Wishes and regrets

1 Point out or elicit the following: *if only* is slightly more emphatic (and less common) than *wish*; more emphatic forms of *it's/it is time* include *it's about time*, *it's high time* and *it really is time*; the *'d* in *I'd rather* is *would*. Give pairs a few minutes to do the task, then go through the answers, eliciting more examples with each of the forms. Explain that we don't use the *would* form (3, 5) in the first person, though we can use *could*, e.g. *I wish I could fly*.

Answers

> **Answers**
>
> **1** wish they would disappear: *would* used after *wish/if only* for regret about a regular habit
> **2** that we considered: past simple after *it is time* meaning 'the time is right for something to happen'
> **3** If only tourists would show: *would* used after *if only/wish* to complain about regular behaviour
> **4** I'd rather my father had been: past perfect for preference about the past
> **5** I wish I could have spent: past modal form for regret about the past
> **6** it is time we changed: simple past after *it's time*
> **7** wished she hadn't looked: past perfect after *wish* for regret about the past
> **8** It's high time you came: simple past after *it's high time*

2 Make it clear that two options are wrong in each case, then give pairs two minutes to do this. Go through the answers.

> **Answers**
>
> **1** had   **2** didn't have   **3** would stop   **4** sought   **5** you'd   **6** could   **7** hadn't spent   **8** were

3 Point out – as with key word transformations – that more than one change will be needed for each of these. Allow about three minutes for students working on their own to write their answers. Then check their work.

> **Answers**
>
> **1** he hadn't told them   **2** you'd/had got/been in   **3** I could speak fluent/I could speak fluently in   **4** realised (that) she needs to make   **5** he hadn't made such a   **6** would stop asking me to lend

4 Point out that there may be several possible answers in each case, but they only need to give two – possibly one each with positive and negative verb forms. Allow five minutes for individuals to write their answers, then check.

> **Suggested answers**
>
> **1** I wish I'd gone to bed earlier. I wish I hadn't stayed up revising so late.
> **2** It's about time you bought a new car. It's high time I got my own car.
> **3** If only I could go there. If only it were cheaper.
> **4** I wish they would stop sending that stuff. I wish they wouldn't keep sending it.
> **5** I'd rather you didn't call round too early. I'd rather you called round a bit later.
> **6** If only I hadn't said that. If only I hadn't been so unkind to her.
> **7** I wish I'd been able to go. I wish I could have gone.
> **8** It's time I got a weekend job. It's time I budgeted my money better.

> See the Workbook and CD-ROM for further practice.

Reading and Use of English

Three-part phrasal verbs

1 Explain that three-part verbs are formed by adding an adverb particle and a preposition to a verb. Give pairs two or three minutes to do these, using dictionaries if necessary, then go through the answers, eliciting more examples with some or all of the phrasal verbs.

> **Answers**
>
> 1 read up on   2 come up against   3 get back to   4 checking up on me   5 brush up on   6 stand up to   7 get through to him   8 did away with

2 Make it clear that the word in A (the adverb) must precede that in B (the preposition), then give pairs three or four minutes to fill in the gaps. Go through the answers, eliciting more examples with the phrasal verbs.

> **Answers**
>
> 1 up to   2 out with   3 down on   4 away from   5 out of   6 round to   7 up with   8 up to

For extra speaking practice, give your students a list of prompts to tell their partner about:

- somebody you look up to
- a rule you would do away with
- people you should stay away from
- something you should cut down on
- a subject you should read up on
- someone you once fell out with
- something you never get round to doing
- something you won't put up with

Tell pairs not to go into too much detail with each of these as the main purpose is to practise the three-part verbs. Quickly elicit some answers after about five minutes.

> **Suggested answers**
>
> 1 I look up to my teacher.   2 They should do away with the rule banning mobile phones in some places.   3 You should stay away from people who steal things.   4 I should cut down on the number of pizzas I eat.   5 I should read up on the history of China.   6 I once fell out with my sister's boyfriend.   7 I never get round to tidying my room.   8 I won't put up with people criticising my friends.

See the Workbook and CD-ROM for further practice.

Part 4

3 Refer the class to the Quick steps and the Exam tip. Tell students to note down their answers to the two initial questions, then work on the exam task on their own for about 12 minutes. Go through the answers when the 12 minutes are up.

> **Answers**
>
> 1 I'd – 1 mark; stay out of – 1 mark
> 2 1 *it's time* + simple past / causative *have/got*   2 three-part phrasal verb   3 would rather + simple past   4 three-part phrasal verb   5 *wish* + simple past / three-part phrasal verb   6 three-part phrasal verb

Exam task

> **Answers**
>
> 1 high time we had / got | the printer   2 hardly any drivers | get away with   3 Mr Jay made | up his mind   4 to talk Jo | out of quitting   5 he hadn't / had not left Lionel | out of   6 come in for | strong criticism

Listening

Personality adjectives

1 Let groups use dictionaries and/or be ready to explain some of the meanings. There will be differences of opinion over how to categorise some of these, so allow plenty of time for discussion. Go through the answers, checking the pronunciation and syllable stress of words such as *conscientious* and *courageous*.

> **Suggested answers**
>
> 1 *Positive*: conscientious, cool, courageous, imaginative, natural, outgoing, trustworthy, well-balanced
> *Negative*: anti-social, insecure, insensitive, naive, narrow-minded, self-centred, self-conscious
> *Either*: extrovert, idealistic, modest, talkative, unconventional
> 2 *Opposites*: anti-social ≠ friendly *or* sociable   conscientious ≠ unconcerned *or* careless   cool ≠ uncool   courageous ≠ cowardly   extrovert ≠ introvert   idealistic ≠ cynical   imaginative ≠ unimaginative   insecure ≠ confident   insensitive ≠ sensitive   modest ≠ boastful *or* proud   naive ≠ sceptical   natural ≠ false *or* affected   narrow-minded ≠ broad-minded   outgoing ≠ shy   self-centred ≠ unselfish   self-conscious ≠ assured *or* self-assured   talkative ≠ quiet *or* reserved   trustworthy ≠ untrustworthy   unconventional ≠ conventional   well-balanced ≠ unwise *or* extreme

2 Put students into pairs. Also encourage the use of the antonyms they came up with, and after about four minutes elicit some answers.

See the Workbook and CD-ROM for further practice.

Part 4

3 Allow 30 seconds for the class to look at the instructions and questions, then elicit the answers.

> **Answers**
>
> Task One focuses on reasons the speakers give for choosing their current occupation; Task Two focuses on personalities

4 Individuals brainstorm words for each of A–H in both tasks. Go through these after they have done the exam task.

5   🔘 2.14   Draw attention to the Quick steps and the Exam tip, then play the recording right through without pausing. When it has finished, allow a few seconds for the class to check they have put an answer to every question and then go through the answers. If you wish, photocopy the script on page 83 for your students and ask them to underline the sections which give the answers.

Exam task

Recording script

Part 4 consists of two tasks. You will hear five short extracts in which people are talking about their jobs and personalities.

Look at Task 1. For questions 1–5, choose from the list (A–H) the reason each speaker gives for choosing their current occupation.

Now look at Task 2. For questions 6–10, choose from the list (A–H) the way each speaker describes their own personality.

While you listen you must complete both tasks. You now have 45 seconds to look at Part 4.

Speaker 1

I seem to spend most of my time defending motorists charged with minor offences instead of (1) <u>fighting for justice for genuine victims of society</u>, as I'd somewhat naively imagined myself doing when I originally applied for this position. But I'd rather be doing that than dealing with paperwork nine-to-five every day because (6) <u>I'm a people person at heart</u>. I'm not one of those over-confident types who starts conversations with everyone in sight, but I do like to chat, and down at the Magistrates court I get to meet clients, witnesses and reporters from the local paper. The salary's not bad, though contrary to the image lawyers sometimes have, that wasn't why I decided to become one.

Speaker 2

I must admit I rarely look ahead in financial terms. (7) <u>I tend to assume I'll either make a loss or at best break even</u>, so usually I end up being pleasantly surprised when neither happens. Not that I ever seriously thought I'd earn more than a basic living when (2) <u>I took this place over from my parents</u>. And I know I should move into bigger premises, but with the unpredictable way the property market has been behaving <u>it would be just my luck to buy just before prices collapsed again</u>, and people cut back on their spending, too. In an ideal world, salaries would go up every year, but that isn't going to happen, is it?

Speaker 3

We're currently in opposition, but there's still plenty to do and meetings until all hours with colleagues. Some of them have very strong views and ideals, and that's fine, (8) <u>but I like to think I'm willing to listen to a wide range of opinions</u>. Actually, I'm going to move on after the next election. (3) <u>It was only ever my intention to spend a few years in the corridors of power before returning to university and applying what I've learnt about politics to some research I want to do</u>. I did both my degrees in business studies and my aim is to compare approaches to management in the political and business spheres. I'm still not sure what I'll do after that.

Speaker 4

Everyone expected me to go into the family business, but even though I left school with pretty good grades there was only ever one thing I wanted to do. Which is this. Not for the material benefits or the lifestyle, but (4) <u>so I could prove to myself that I can actually compete at this level</u>. I may not be quite as gifted as some, (9) <u>so I try to make up for it by putting in as much time and effort as I can on the training ground to perfect my skills</u>. Next weekend, we've got an away game that some of my team mates expect to lose, though I'm a little more optimistic about it.

Speaker 5

I've got a degree in politics so I love covering political stories, especially when a general election is close and the candidates are desperately trying to use us to get their message across to the public. One of my colleagues later went on to become a successful politician himself, a minister in fact. (10) <u>And I must admit that kind of appeals to me, too, so I'm making as many contacts as I can</u>. It'd certainly be an improvement on what I'm currently doing, which consists of working nine-to-five drafting copy on the private lives of celebrities rather than (5) <u>writing anything original or imaginative, which was what initially attracted me to journalism</u>.

See the Workbook for further practice.

Speaking

Reaching a decision

1   Remind the class that after two minutes of Part 3, the examiner will ask them to reach a decision together, for example about which of the things they have been discussing is the most important, and that they will then have a minute to do this. Give pairs two or three minutes to do the matching, then elicit more ways of expressing some or all of 1–5.

Parts 3 & 4

2   Give pairs a minute to look at the task, then ask the class for the answer. Refer students to page 109 of the Speaking guide.

3 ⊙ *2.15* Point out that they will hear the decision-making section only, not the whole task. Play the recording once through without pausing, then ask the class for the answer.

Answers

1 taking regular breaks from work or study   **2** yes

Recording script

Teacher: Now you have about a minute to decide which method would be the most effective in helping people reduce everyday stress.

Alina: OK, which shall we have?

Ivan: I think I'd go for taking regular breaks. If you do that you can avoid getting all stressed out when you're revising, or doing some kind of work.

Alina: But don't you think there's a risk of taking longer and longer breaks until eventually you're not doing enough studying or work or whatever, and then you end up getting worried about that?

Ivan: I can see what you mean, but if you keep the breaks to no more than, say five or ten minutes each hour, you should be all right. In fact, you'll probably find you actually get more work done overall than without the breaks, simply because you're not getting so tired.

Alina: OK, taking breaks. As long as they're short.

Ivan: So we're agreed, then.

Alina: Yes.

---

4 ⊙ *2.15* Play the recording once or twice more, pausing if necessary for students to make notes. Go through the answers, suggesting they use some of these expressions when they do the decision-making part of the exam task.

Answers

OK, which shall we have?   I think I'd go for…
But don't you think…   So we're agreed, then.

5 Time the activity so that it lasts no longer than three minutes in total (you may want to indicate when the first two minutes are up).

6 The class play the roles of 'examiner' and 'candidates'. Remind the candidates that they can ask for repetition of the questions, but the examiners cannot rephrase or add to the printed questions apart from adding the prompts given in the bullet points. Groups could begin simultaneously so that you can ensure that each Part 4 lasts about five minutes. Remind groups to be polite and constructive in their comments. Finish with a class round-up, asking what difficulties were encountered and making a note of these for future classwork.

Writing

Concession

1 Explain that a concession clause gives information that contrasts with that in the main clause, or is unexpected in some way. Some of the expressions used to do this, e.g. *despite*, were introduced in Contrast links in Unit 1. Tell the class that some of the concession links in this exercise (e.g. *whichever*) can stand alone, while others (e.g. *how*) form part of fixed phrases. Give pairs two minutes to note down their answers, then check and elicit more examples with each.

Answers

1 (no matter) how   **2** (Even) so   **3** may   **4** (no matter) who
5 (all the) same   **6** whichever   **7** (and) yet   **8** wherever

2 Point that there may be more than one possible answer for some of these, including changing the order of clauses. Give individuals about three minutes to do these, then check their answers, eliciting other possibilities.

Suggested answers

1 Whatever you say, I won't change my mind.
2 Jessica was obviously exhausted by then. Even so, she carried on working.
3 No matter where you go, this phone lets you stay in touch.
4 I still think it's a boring series, however wonderful the TV critics say it is.
5 Ethan James is a brilliant artist, and yet nobody's heard of him.
6 The talk was rather long. All the same, the speaker made some good points.
7 Max may be unable to recall names, but he has an excellent memory for numbers.
8 Amy will keep on doing what she feels is right, no matter what people say.

3 Point out that they may find some of the forms they practise in this exercise useful when they come to write their essay. Get individuals to note down their answers, then check and elicit some of these.

Suggested answers

1 they may live.   **2** what their background.   **3** in fact often make silly mistakes.   **4** they may develop into totally different people.   **5** many have had successful careers.   **6** old they are.

See the Workbook for further practice.

Part 1: essay

4 Give the class a minute to look at the task, then elicit the answers.

Answers

1 factors that help determine an individual's personality
2 genetics, family life, society in general
3 which you think is more important, giving reasons.

5 Give students working on their own two to three minutes to decide on their answers. Then ask which they have chosen, why, and what is wrong with the other two.

> **Answers**
>
> Paragraph A states the topic and indicates the content, but it uses much the same language as the instructions.
> Paragraph B (the best) paraphrases the language used in the instructions and states the two main points that will be discussed in the essay.
> Paragraph C defines the key term, paraphrases part of the instructions and focuses on the main issue, but fails to indicate the content of the essay beyond that.

6 Give pairs five minutes to study the text and note down their answers. Take any vocabulary questions as you go through the answers.

> **Answers**
>
> **1** genetics 3rd paragraph, society in general 2nd paragraph
> **2** "Just as physical characteristics…" → *our DNA not only determines attributes like our height or life expectancy, it also affects traits such as how open, extrovert or conscientious we are.*
> "School life has…" → *Of particular importance is the school environment, where the child's way of interacting, their response to rules and how they are treated by others all help shape their character.*
> **3** Society in general, because siblings can differ so much in personality, and a sense of humour has to be learned.
> **4** *no matter what our environment; we may have inborn characteristics and abilities, but; however similar their DNA*

7 Students brainstorm these points on their own in four to five minutes. Encourage them also to come up with their own ideas.

8 Remind students about the Quick steps and refer them to the Exam tip. Refer them also to page 99 of the Writing guide. Allow the class 35 minutes for writing, as they are already familiar with the task and have made notes for their essay. Then give them five minutes to check their own work.

Model answer

Personality, the sum of all the qualities that together form an individual's distinctive character, is shaped by many forces. Chief among these are the home environment and the social environment.

A child begins life interacting with its parents, brothers or sisters and possibly also grandparents, and these relationships lead to the development of its emotions, both positive and negative. Parents may also encourage or discourage qualities such as sociability, a desire to learn and self-confidence, and also affect the child's developing personality by being authoritarian or tolerant, critical or supportive. They also act as role models, with the result that their child often acquires many of the same character traits.

The social environment includes school life, where the child meets a much wider range of personality types and has to cope with different kinds of relationships, both with peers and adults. Its response to these has a major effect on its personality. As the child grows up, society beyond school becomes a growing influence, especially now that young people can so easily use social media to make new friends, no matter where they live.

Overall, I believe the role of the family has been overestimated. Studies indicate that twins brought up apart have much more similar personalities than random pairs of people, and that by adulthood biological siblings remain far more alike than adoptive siblings. Moreover, the family structure is changing, with young people spending much less time talking to a parent or sibling than interacting online. That, increasingly, is how personality is formed.

See the Workbook and CD-ROM for further practice.

Writing guide answer key

Part 1

1 1 The number of elderly people is increasing, and that has implications for many aspects of daily life.

2 ways of meeting the needs of an ageing population

3 your tutor

2 1 formal: complex sentences (most sentences consist of two or three clauses, e.g. the first sentence); linking expressions such as 'In connection with', 'Such activity' (both in the third paragraph) and 'Nevertheless' (last paragraph); words like 'presents' (first paragraph), 'impaired' (second paragraph)

2 introduction – relevant background information; care homes; work; conclusion

3 residential care homes

Part 2

Letter

1 1 an English friend

2 how people's lives have changed in your country over the last few decades

3 describe improvements in people's lives, and anything that is worse now

2 1 It's very appropriate as it's informal – vocabulary (e.g. 'Great', 'chat'), use of first person, contracted verb forms (e.g. 'you're')

2 yes: it starts with social remarks, goes on to improvements, mentions something that's worse, rounds off the letter

3 third to fifth paragraphs – improvements; sixth paragraph – something that's worse now

Report

1 1 company's sponsorship of a local sports club

2 your manager

3 explain why the company chose to sponsor that club; describe the form that the sponsorship takes; suggest with reasons why it should or should not continue

2 1 formal – passive verb forms, complex sentences, impersonal tone

2 Reasons for sponsorship – why your company chose to sponsor that sports club; Details of sponsorship – what form the sponsorship takes; Recommendation – suggest with reasons why it should or should not continue

3 to continue to sponsor the football club

Proposal

1 1 improving contact between foreign students and local residents

2 the town council

3 outline problems with the present situation and suggest how it could be improved

2 1 neutral to formal (the use of the first person makes this less formal than the report above): complex sentences; 'there is little social contact' (second paragraph), rather than the informal 'there isn't much social contact'; 'I suggest that' (in 'Recommendation' section), rather than an informal structure starting 'Why don't you' or 'How about'

2 Present situation – outlining problems with the present situation; Recommendation – suggesting how it could be improved

3 to start cookery classes run by students and local residents

Review

1 1 a restaurant

2 a local magazine; local residents and visitors interested in eating in restaurants

3 explain why you had particular expectations of the restaurant; how your experience compared with what you expected

2 1 last paragraph (last sentence)

2 first and second paragraphs

3 first paragraph

Photocopiable recording script

Unit 1, Listening, Part 4

Speaker 1

As I looked across the countryside, I saw that distinctive shape sweeping across the distant fields and then over the surface of the lake, which at that time of the year was of course full. There it picked up huge quantities of water and then continued overland on its way. It could have gone in any direction, but I'd had a strange feeling that it was coming after me and sure enough it kept on heading my way, closer and closer. I'd been expecting it to make a really deafening sound but what struck me was the way it twisted across the open flat farmland in virtual silence, and somehow that made it even more alarming.

Speaker 2

It was when I reached a point overlooking the valley that I saw it gradually moving east far below me, consuming everything in its path as such intense ones always do. It was quite a scary sight, though when I thought about it rationally it seemed highly unlikely it would suddenly alter course and put me in danger. But when it reached the bushes at the foot of the hill where I was standing, that was exactly what happened. Fuelled by the dry vegetation on the steep slope, it began racing towards me and I fled back down the way I'd come to safety. Later I was told they tend to accelerate when they spread uphill, on other occasions reaching homes on higher ground with tragic results.

Speaker 3

I suppose I should have been shocked when I saw for myself just how many square miles it covered, and how dense were the clouds of smoke where attempts were being made to burn it off, but having previously studied satellite photos I knew pretty much what to expect. I still, though, felt deep sadness at the immense harm that sticky mess was causing to wildlife, both above and beneath the surface. That feeling wasn't helped by my travelling companion reminding me of the depressing statistics in such cases, but what really shook me was the figure he quoted for the frequency of such disasters, the majority of which the media are either unaware of or choose to ignore. Apparently it runs into dozens, every month.

Speaker 4

My friend Lauren and I were out walking in the hills on a hot, sunny day when we noticed a kind of trembling under our feet, rather like when you're standing on a bridge and a lorry goes past. But there were no vehicles in sight, no road or rail tunnels below us – and the nearest volcano was half a continent away. Then Lauren said she'd seen a local press report about an oil company pumping liquid underground to extract oil and gas, which caused huge sections of the rock to suddenly shift below that part of the countryside. So that was the explanation, as apparently even the really major ones can be pretty quiet. I was speechless.

Speaker 5

I'd heard warnings on the radio so I was half-expecting something like this to happen here, but destruction on this kind of scale was not something I'd envisaged. Trapped on the roof, I surveyed the dreadful scene around me. Local landmarks such as the flower gardens were unrecognisable, and when eventually they reappeared they would be covered in thick black mud. Much worse, though, would be the effect on people's homes, where possessions would be soaked and ruined. Other houses were burning, no doubt because of electrical appliances left switched on. I did spot two firefighters rowing along a street, but their priority was to take the very young and the very old to safety, not to try to put out fires.

Unit 1, Speaking, Part 1, Exercise 4

Teacher: OK, Cristina. Where are you from?

Cristina: I'm from Getafe, which is quite a big town about ten kilometres to the south of Madrid.

Teacher: What do you do there?

Cristina: I'm a student. I've been studying information technology at the university of Móstoles since about two years ago.

Teacher: What do you think you'll be doing in five years' time?

Cristina: Can you repeat that, please?

Teacher: What do you think you'll be doing in five years' time?

Cristina: Er, it's hard to say, really, but I hope very much I'll be working in a big company. Maybe abroad because it is very difficult to find a job in Spain, even with a degree.

Teacher: How important do you think it is to speak more than one language?

Cristina: It's definitely very important, especially English. And if you speak both Spanish and English you can have many opportunities in the future, in the western part of the world anyway.

Teacher: OK, Markus. Where are you from?

Markus: I grew up in Hamburg.

Teacher: What do you most enjoy about learning English?

Markus: The grammar. It is relatively simple, I think.

Teacher: Do you prefer to get the news from television, newspapers or the Internet?

Markus: The Internet.

Teacher: Why?

Markus: You can compare, er, sources of news. In many cases, they report the same story in completely different ways.

Teacher: What would you do if you suddenly became very rich?

Markus: I would buy a house. I'd like to have an extremely large garden.

Compact Advanced by Peter May ©Cambridge University Press and UCLES 2014

Unit 2, Listening, Part 2

The Peruvian city of Cuzco is a total experience, from its location 11,000 feet up in the Andes mountains, its history as the ancient capital of the Inca Empire and its unique culture, to the blend of Inca and Spanish architecture from different centuries that has led to researchers referring to it as an open-air museum.

Its origins actually go back over a thousand years, but it was in the 13th century that the invading Incas reached Cuzco. They planned and built the city so that it resembled a mountain lion, and districts and individual streets still bear the names of body parts such as the head and back, while the tail was formed by straightening the point where two rivers joined.

Although night-time temperatures in Cuzco can be quite mild, that is certainly not the case all year round. On account of that, many of the original Inca homes there lacked windows and had just a single door, which would have been covered by a thick mat during the chillier months. There would also have been a straw roof that had to be replaced every few years.

My colleagues and I were there in late June, and I noticed on the first afternoon that a number of the others were looking distinctly uncomfortable as the fierce sun began to beat down, but as an Australian I'm accustomed to that. The height above sea level was another matter, leaving all of us short of breath at times, especially when climbing the steep hills around the city.

Having arrived a couple of days ahead of the Festival of the Sun, we were able to watch some of the performers practising for the big day. What really stood out for me was the folk dancing, though some of the concerts and parades were well worth watching, too.

On the 24th, the day of the Festival itself, the city centre was packed as the procession set off. The multi-coloured costumes were fabulous, even more varied than I'd imagined, as the participants moved slowly up the hill to the ancient site called Saksaywaman where the main ceremony would take place.

That is where the magnificent walls are located. Standing nearly six metres tall and measuring up to 400 metres in length, they were built of huge stones that fitted together perfectly. Given that some of them weighed 200 tons each, the only way the Incas could have achieved that, my research indicates, is by sculpting models in lighter materials to the exact size and shape required, and then reproducing them in stone.

I stood there marvelling at the sight of the walls, and at the colourful scene as the ceremony began. Looking at the vast crowds of spectators, I recalled a paper written by a local historian which made the point that in Inca times there weren't any. In one way or another, all the thousands of people at the Festival in those days were participants.

Compact Advanced by Peter May ©Cambridge University Press and UCLES 2014

Unit 3, Listening, Part 1

Extract one

You hear a couple, Jack and Emily, discussing a problem he has at work.

Now look at questions one and two.

F: So what happened? I thought you two got on well?

M: We used to, yes. But when he heard last week that the new contract had been assigned to me, he suddenly stopped speaking, and today he started a row when he saw me in the canteen. At one point it got so heated he threatened to take it up with the general manager, though I knew he wouldn't actually go that far. Any more than he'd walk out on the job, as at one point he said he might.

F: I suppose in a way you can understand why he's so upset. He's been there longer than you, after all. But I know he can be quite aggressive, so rather than try to discuss it rationally with him I think I'd do my utmost to keep out of his way until he calms down a little. I'd certainly find somewhere else to eat, or a different time. When does he usually have lunch?

M: Twelve-thirty.

F: So how about having lunch at noon, for the time being at least?

M: That makes sense, yes.

Extract two

You hear two people discussing a news story that they have just watched on TV.

Now look at questions three and four.

M: That was quite interesting, wasn't it? Particularly the bit about eye contact. So, looking straight at you says nothing at all about whether someone's telling you the truth or not.

F: Yes, I've always thought that was a myth. It's not as if cleverer liars were unaware some people believe that, and I'm sure some criminals try it on. Though, as the reporter said, the police aren't fooled, they just ignore it.

M: But the effective ways of spotting liars – I liked some of those used by detectives, such as noticing how quickly people answer a question.

F: Yes, it's logical they'll take longer to reply if they're having to invent a complicated story. And also getting suspects to give their version of events in reverse order. It'd never occurred to me before, but that must be much harder if you're making it up as you go along.

M: And what did you think of the figure quoted for the number of lies the average person admits to telling each day? About one and a half, wasn't it?

F: Yeah, though I suspect some of them might have been lying about how often they lie!

Extract three

You hear two students, Amelia and Ollie, in a café talking about flat sharing.

Now look at questions five and six.

M: So after all the flat sharing we've done over the last couple of years, what lessons do you think we've learned?

F: The crucial thing is the initial choice of people. Because if you don't take your time doing that, you can end up with all kinds of tensions. What you really want is a relaxed relationship with the others, and also the hope – especially if you're new in town – that they'll take you out to places and help you socialise.

M: I suppose you might get lucky and hit it off with the first ones you meet, and if they happen to be sociable types, you'll get to hang out with their mates, too – but more often it's about making compromises with acquaintances, isn't it?

F: It's certainly true you have to compromise when it comes to keeping the place clean. I think I have pretty high standards of hygiene and I wouldn't share with anyone – male or female – who was really messy, but I don't think there's any need to make a fuss about trivial things. I mean, it's a real pain if some perfectionist starts complaining just because, say, you leave the odd mug in the sink.

Compact Advanced by Peter May ©Cambridge University Press and UCLES 2014

Unit 4, Listening, Part 3

Interviewer:	My guest today is Liam Callaghan, a second-year history undergraduate who had some difficulties managing money when he went to university. So Liam, as a student suddenly living on your own in another city, I suppose the first thing you had to do was set up a bank account. How did you decide which bank to choose?
Liam:	I'd already arranged a student loan and to be honest my only concern was getting my hands on the cash as easily as possible. All the main banks had branches on campus which meant any of them would do. And I wasn't bothered about things like how much they'd let you borrow on a credit card, or whether they'd let you overdraw without having to pay interest. So it came down to what they were giving away in an attempt to attract people like me. In the end, I opted for the one offering the clock radio in the hope it would get me up in the mornings, though it wasn't very successful in that respect.
Int:	And how did you get on managing your finances? Did you find having a student card made things much cheaper?
Liam:	Yes and no. Things like cut-price tickets to see films are fine if that's what you like doing, but I'd rather stay at home with a take-away meal on my lap as I watch DVDs. Now they *are* something you can make quite a saving on, with some websites giving a percentage off if you're in full-time education. The same goes for textbooks and other stuff you need. I also saved a lot on long-distance coach fares, much more than going by train. People talk about how a student railcard can save you money, but the fact is you get a better deal by booking your tickets in advance, like everyone else.
Int:	Did you go home during the holidays, or stay in the hall of residence?
Liam:	I went home at Easter, though unfortunately while I was away my room was broken into, and my laptop stolen.
Int:	Really?
Liam:	Yes, I shouldn't have left valuables there, I realise that now. Especially as they weren't insured. I'd assumed they'd be covered by my parents' policy because I'd got them to extend their contents insurance to cover my things while I was away, but when I tried to claim I was told it only applied during term time. The laptop was the biggest loss, both financially and in terms of losing all the study notes I had on it, not that they'd be any use to anyone else even if they could access the files. A friend asked me why it was so easy for them to get into my room, but the truth is there's not much you can do to keep determined thieves out when almost everybody's away.
Int:	That must have been a shock for you. Did you have to replace the laptop yourself?
Liam:	Yes, and it was at that point I noticed I was spending too much overall. It wasn't that I was splashing out on suits or shoes or anything like that, or going to expensive nightclubs and restaurants. Actually, if my friends and I did go out, we'd usually just have a coffee somewhere and share a cab home, which actually worked out cheaper than taking the bus. No, what was taking me over budget was paying back some cash I'd borrowed a few months earlier. I'd got it from one of those money shops without working out the true interest rate.
Int:	So now you owed money. How did you feel about that?
Liam:	Well, in situations like that it's always easy to say somebody should've warned you, but really I had no-one else to blame but myself. I also knew that my family weren't in a financial position to come to my rescue so it was up to me to sort it out. I didn't doubt my ability to do so as long as the people I owed money to kept their side of the agreement, and I had no reason to believe they wouldn't. It all worked out in the end, but it wasn't an experience I'd care to repeat.
Int:	What would you advise other students in that situation to do?
Liam:	Firstly, to face up to reality. There's no way the debt will go away and there's no chance of talking lenders into charging you less interest on it, so all you can do is find out the minimum amount they'll accept over how many months, make a deal on that basis and stick to it. There's always a temptation to relieve the pressure by borrowing elsewhere and paying that back over a longer period, but all you're doing then is prolonging the situation. Of course, to reduce any debt you've got to cut back on your spending, though I wouldn't recommend going without essentials. Yes, you have to economise – but don't forget to eat.
Int:	Liam Callaghan, many thanks.

Unit 5, Listening, Part 2

When you tell people you're studying to be a doctor, they sometimes ask whether your family first suggested it to you, but although my parents are delighted that I'm now a medical student, I don't think they ever mentioned it back then. The only one who did, I think, was a classmate who I'd given first aid to after she'd got hurt in the gym. I think the gym teacher was quite impressed and she too may have felt that I might become a doctor, but if so she kept it to herself.

Actually none of the other staff ever suggested it to me as a possible career, either. On reflection, they probably considered I lacked the academic ability necessary to do a degree in medicine. I think I can prove them wrong about that, though it's certainly one of the longest and most demanding degree courses.

But that wasn't what I first did at university. I'd always liked science subjects and when I was seventeen I had to make my mind up which courses I wanted to apply for. For a while I was considering doing I.T. but in the end I had to face up to the fact that maths wasn't one of my strong points; unlike chemistry, which I'd always been reasonably good at, and that's what I decided to do.

I enjoyed my time at university and in the main found the course interesting, but I knew I wasn't suited to doing chemical research and after graduation I started work as a research assistant at the local medical centre. There I came into contact with doctors for the first time, and listening to them it soon became apparent to me that the job satisfaction they feel is of a kind experienced in no other profession. Other careers may offer the high salary, the respect of other people or the lifelong opportunity to keep learning, but not that.

I then did some work experience at a local nursing home, which gave me a real insight into the world of health care. Helping the patients there was immensely rewarding and I wished I could have done more for them, though of course my medical knowledge at that time was far too limited for me to do so.

Motivated by this experience I did some studying in my spare time, and six months later I felt ready to take the admissions test required by medical schools. I also attended open days at several of them. I'd assumed that I would learn most from the staff there, and although talking to them was certainly worthwhile, it was what current students had to say that really made an impression on me, and helped me make my mind up which place would suit me best.

Eventually I sent off my application form, stating my choice of school. I heard nothing for quite some time and I was half expecting a rejection, but then I received a message – an email I think it was – asking me to go for an interview. And then, finally, that unforgettable moment when the acceptance letter popped through the door. I immediately texted all my friends, inviting them to a celebration party.

I'm about halfway through my course now, well aware that I still have an enormous amount to learn before I can even begin to think of myself as a doctor, but I do have some tentative ideas for the future. I want to spend the first few years in a local hospital, perhaps working in A & E, and maybe then do a PhD at a specialist hospital. But ultimately what I'd most like to do is apply my medical knowledge and skills to helping those where the need is greatest: the developing countries. One of the great attractions of medicine as a career is that it offers enormous flexibility, and opportunities to make a difference to the lives of some of the most vulnerable people on Earth.

Compact Advanced by Peter May ©Cambridge University Press and UCLES 2014

Unit 5, Speaking, Part 2

Teacher: Zeinab, it's your turn first. Here are your pictures. They show people winning Olympic medals. Compare two of the pictures, and say how difficult it might have been for them to acquire the skills needed to reach this level, and how these people might be feeling.

Zeinab: Well, they both show people competing in Olympic events. All three must have trained very hard to get to this standard because you have to be extremely fit either to be a gymnast or to sail this kind of boat. I'd say, though, that becoming a top gymnast takes a lot more practice in terms of balance and timing. On the other hand, the women in the boat have to learn to work closely together, to coordinate everything, so this isn't an individual sport like gymnastics. They're also racing against others at the same time, with the risk of collision, while the gymnast does his turn completely alone. That means, though, he's probably feeling very nervous right now, especially as the crowd and his opponents are all watching, waiting for him to make the slightest mistake. The sailors are possibly feeling less nervous than him, not least because there's nobody else around.

Teacher: Reza, who do you think has put the most effort into acquiring their skills?

Reza: Sorry, could you say that again, please?

Teacher: Who do you think has put the most effort into acquiring their skills?

Reza: My own feeling is that it's probably the relay runner. He's had to train as hard as a top sprinter in terms of fitness and becoming one of the fastest men in the world. He's also had to practise getting up to exactly the same speed as the incoming runner within the regulation distance, as well as the technique of taking the baton correctly and at just the right time. Because if he drops it, or impedes any of his opponents or breaks any of the other rules, his whole team will be disqualified.

Teacher: Thank you.

Unit 6, Listening, Part 4

Speaker 1

Woman: Actually, I'd already seen the film version so there weren't any real plot surprises, but I was in one of the front rows and overall it was a reasonably enjoyable couple of hours. To be honest I wasn't expecting it to be up to much after what the critics had said about it, but at times I found myself wondering whether they'd actually seen the same thing as me. How one of them could say, for instance, that they felt 'thoroughly bored throughout' remains a mystery to me. In future I'll take a little less notice of the reviews, not just of drama but of exhibitions and opera, too.

Speaker 2

Man: There was certainly some rather clever photography, especially in the urban locations, and the soundtrack featuring some original songs was above average, too. But, as I'd read in a review somewhere, it was clear that the plot lacked originality, and before long the thought of having to put up with an entire box set of it literally had me yawning. My friends, though, seemed to find it quite absorbing so I had no option but to sit through the whole thing, wishing all the time I'd managed to persuade them to switch on that live broadcast of classical music instead.

Speaker 3

Woman: I was immediately struck by the craftsmanship, the skill and the dedication that must have gone into producing them. Some could have passed for photographs, they were that realistic, while others were so striking I couldn't take my eyes off them. That of course was why they'd been produced in the first place, from the time of the revolution and then up to and including the next great conflict. I imagined them stuck on walls and in railways stations as terrifying events took place, and could feel the immense power of the messages they must have conveyed at the time. I would have taken some photos but of course it isn't allowed there.

Speaker 4

Man: I'd gone along after seeing posters advertising the event, and I wasn't disappointed. Although shot in the so-called golden hour near the end of the day when shadows are softer, the images shine a harsh light on the reality of living in one of the most deprived parts of the country. Striking in their simplicity, and without accompanying notes as they speak for themselves, they capture the sense of utter hopelessness felt by people living in those conditions, leaving me with much the same feeling. My spirits sank even further when I thought about how little present-day society seems to care. We don't even make documentaries or films about them anymore.

Speaker 5

Woman: We'd been looking forward to our afternoon there, but it was a real let-down, almost amateurish in fact. There was an almost total lack of information, the facilities were poorly maintained and there were virtually no exhibits of any significance. A friendly but clueless member of staff explained that the most interesting objects were out on loan to the archaeology department of the university, and suggested we could see them being dug up in what he called 'the film'. This turned out to be a poor-quality video shown on an old TV, so we didn't bother. We might just have found all this amusing, but for the fact that we could have been at the theatre with friends instead.

Compact Advanced by Peter May ©Cambridge University Press and UCLES 2014

Unit 6, Speaking, Part 1

Teacher: What do you like doing online?

Olga: I enjoy reading articles. And emailing people.

Teacher: Do you prefer to watch films on TV or at the cinema?

Olga: I don't really mind. But if it's a new film with lots of action, then I prefer to see it on a big, er, screen. With my friends.

Teacher: What do you like to do in your spare time?

Nikos: Well, whenever I get a moment to myself I like to read. I'm really keen on science fiction.

Teacher: Do you prefer to listen to pop music or to folk music?

Nikos: Sorry, could you say that again?

Teacher: Do you prefer to listen to pop music or to folk music?

Nikos: I don't think I've ever thought about that before, but I suppose most of the time I'd rather listen to pop, if it's good of course. Though I enjoy hearing the traditional music of my country, too. Especially on social occasions like weddings.

Unit 7, Listening, Part 1

Extract One

You overhear two colleagues talking about the man's recent holiday.

Now look at questions one and two.

M: Higher up on the main slopes there was far less than in previous years; in fact there were huge bare patches on some of them. It must have put a lot of other people off, too. The whole resort area is usually quite crowded but this time there was hardly a soul in sight, even though all the hotel prices were heavily discounted. So all in all it was something of a wasted trip, really.

F: Well, I think I'd have counted myself lucky just to be somewhere that beautiful at this time of year! But if what you saw there is part of a more general pattern, and it does seem the same thing's been happening in mountainous areas in other parts of the world, then it looks as though we're seeing the physical results of climate change sooner than we expected even just a few years ago.

M: Or maybe it's just a temporary thing, as some people claim. Periods of warm and cold weather go in cycles, don't they?

F: To some extent, certainly. But I think we're looking at a longer-term trend now.

Extract Two

You hear two friends discussing a documentary programme about a tropical rainforest.

Now look at questions three and four.

F: It was over-ambitious, really, wasn't it? I mean, trying to pack into 40 minutes the entire evolution of the rainforests, the range of trees, plants and animals in them, plus all the danger they're now in. It's just not possible.

M: I don't think I could have sat through any more of that, to be honest. Especially with the narrator talking to viewers as if they were schoolkids. It was like being back in biology lessons. He sounded like he'd never done a voice-over before.

F: Actually, I thought he had quite a pleasant voice, though I must admit I could have done without it whenever I was trying to listen to all those marvellous background sounds: the birds and monkeys and everything.

M: I've seen better camera work, too. At times that looked more like a home video.

F: There were some nice shots, though. Especially those taken from above the tree tops.

M: Yes, they were very much the exceptions, and they must've paid some actual professionals quite a lot to get those. Though they could have saved all that money by filming it in Cairns, in north-east Australia. There's a cable car near there that runs right above the rainforest.

Extract Three

You hear part of an interview with a woman called Anne Murphy, who is campaigning against the building of a new factory.

Now look at questions five and six.

Int: Anne, can you tell us why you're so opposed to this scheme?

Anne: Quite simply it's a local beauty spot, and whoever had the idea of putting a food processing factory in those lovely green fields right next to the river simply doesn't care how much damage it would do. I know the plan includes an effective water treatment plant, but such a large development would be impossible without new roads, power lines and so on, with all the harm that would do to the countryside.

Int: And what do the farmers say about this?

Anne: Well, there's a lot of compensation on offer and they're likely to take it. Actually, they've now said that if this scheme doesn't go ahead they'll find another buyer for the land, so doing nothing with it isn't an option, either. Finding an alternative use for it, perhaps as a country park or something like that, sounds like the best bet. I know that some of the people on the town council have argued for going ahead with the plan on a slightly reduced scale, but that's completely out of the question as far I'm concerned.

Compact Advanced by Peter May ©Cambridge University Press and UCLES 2014

Unit 7, Speaking, Part 3

Aishar: So how do you feel about this one?

Haziq: I think it's a good idea.

Aishar: Any particular reason?

Haziq: Well, a lot of people throw out clothes they've only worn a couple of times, which is a terrible waste.

Aishar: That's a good point.

Haziq: So instead of doing that they could put them, say, in one of those things you see in the street for used clothes.

Aishar: Right, I know the ones you mean. Or you could take them to a charity shop, Oxfam for instance, who sell them to raise money. Either way someone gets to wear them, free or at a lower price.

Haziq: Yes, and that means they don't become waste.

Aishar: OK, the next one. What are your thoughts on this?

Unit 8, Listening, Part 2

It's a fabulous job to have, though when I was turned down by the Air Force I thought I'd never actually be a pilot. I had the right degree, I performed well in the psychological test and my general fitness level was fine, but it was my eyesight that let me down. It just didn't meet the standards required for flying combat aircraft. Fortunately, though, I was accepted for training at a civilian flying school.

To become a pilot there's a huge amount to learn, from physics and meteorology to navigation and understanding aircraft systems. And even when you qualify it's highly unlikely your first job will be as a regular pilot. You'll probably be a reserve pilot, waiting on call at or near an airport rather like passengers on standby – except that you'll have to be on the plane within 90 minutes to help fly it.

There are normally two pilots on the flight deck: the captain and the first officer. Some older aircraft might also have a flight engineer, though as happened with radio operators and navigators several decades ago they're being replaced by technology, in this case by computers.

The working hours aren't bad, with around 14 days a month off. Though for someone like me who's currently flying between Europe and South America, some of those are inevitably spent far from home. For international flights you can be on duty up to sixteen hours, of which twelve are the most you can spend continuously at the controls, whereas for domestic routes the maximum is eight hours without a break.

Naturally, you particularly enjoy landing in certain places. Some because you're arriving in warm sunny weather in the southern hemisphere when it's gloomy midwinter in the north, while at others it's the great views you get from the flight deck window, especially in Switzerland, say.

For some pilots the downside is the testing that takes place twice a year, throughout your career. And if you're not up to scratch, you're out of a job. It's as simple as that and I don't have a problem with it. I know that as in any profession there's always room for improvement, so whenever I receive criticism I try to learn from it, knowing that what is said is always meant constructively.

In many ways I'm fortunate to have this job. Few pilots are taken on by major airlines and fewer still reach senior positions where they may earn a hundred thousand a year. Not long ago this airline had three thousand applications when they advertised twenty-five posts. They were all from qualified pilots.

And even if you are taken on, job security is not great. Major airlines have been known to go out of business, and any ups or downs in the economic situation tend to have a disproportionate effect on the airline industry. Routes may be cut and aircraft orders cancelled. So if you're thinking of a career as a pilot, choose your airline carefully – then stick with it.

Compact Advanced by Peter May ©Cambridge University Press and UCLES 2014

Unit 8, Speaking, Part 4

Teacher: Maxim, do you think people should choose a career when they are very young?

Maxim: I'm sorry, could you repeat that?

Teacher: Do you think people should choose a career when they are very young?

Maxim: It's hard to say. You could argue that the people who do best in life are the ones who decide at an early age what they want to do and then get on and work towards that. But given that most people will probably have more than one career as society changes and technology develops, some would say there's no real hurry. So maybe what matters is being able to acquire skills when they become necessary, rather than trying to make plans now for an uncertain future.

Teacher: Do you agree, Dariya?

Dariya: To a certain extent, yes, but I do think it's the young people who already know they want to be doctors, lawyers, teachers and so on who will ultimately be the most successful, particularly as they'll be in professions that will always be needed. And I don't think they'll ever be replaced by computers, either.

Unit 9, Listening, Part 3

Interviewer: Good morning from the conference centre, where the Science Fair is taking place. It's an annual event designed to give young people the opportunity to learn more about the scientific process through experimentation, problem solving, and in-depth learning. With me is Kieran Shaw, a Physics teacher accompanying his students. Tell me, Kieran, what do you think of this fair compared to that of previous years?

Kieran: It's excellent, certainly up to last year's already high standards as far as the projects themselves are concerned, and with the same number entered, which I think is about right. I just hope they manage to avoid last year's row over the final choice of winners, which was controversial to say the least. There's a different panel this time and that should make a difference, but there's no change in their policy of awarding three prizes in each category, and I think that also makes sense.

Interviewer: You say the numbers taking part here have held up, but is that the case in other fairs?

Kieran: Not everywhere, no. And I'm a little worried that we might start to see fewer people taking part in them generally.

Interviewer: Is that because of the economic situation, with schools having to make cutbacks?

Kieran: In most cases it costs schools little or nothing for students to attend, so that's unlikely to be a factor, and neither is the expense involved in developing and presenting the projects, which most students' families find reasonably affordable. Of more concern is the feeling in some quarters that actually going somewhere to see science in action belongs to the pre-internet era, though the majority of the students themselves seem as keen as ever to attend fairs despite the fact that it usually means giving up a Saturday to do so!

Interviewer: There are also some issues surrounding the fairs themselves, aren't there?

Kieran: Yes, one of the key ones being the traditional male dominance of science subjects, leading to girls being under-represented in these projects – though happily there's a good gender balance across my groups. They're also good at working in and between groups, so there isn't the over-competitive atmosphere that some people complain about. A more valid point is that someone whose father, say, is a chemist may not be doing all the work themselves, and I have had to look into to one or two cases like that. It's also sometimes alleged that those from wealthy backgrounds can afford to go for more complex projects, but I think there's a good socio-economic mix in each of my groups, too.

Interviewer: So what's the main criterion when selecting a topic? Its originality?

Kieran: Well, that's certainly a factor to take into account, but first and foremost it must be something capable of holding the participants' attention over the months leading up to the fair. Avoiding areas that might be too complicated for young students to explain clearly in their presentation matters, too – as, by the way, does anything that may require spending a lot on apparatus – but not to the same extent.

Interviewer: How do students get on doing their presentations? I imagine some are pretty nervous.

Kieran: Yes, and to overcome their nerves some of them try to learn everything off by heart and then make a speech to the judges, which of course isn't how it works. The judges will look at the display and perhaps briefly at their notes, and then ask them some questions. It's important they don't rush their answers, but it's also best to keep them simple, avoiding any jargon they're unable to explain if asked to by the judges. That happens quite often, and doesn't give a good impression. The important thing is knowing what everything in their notes means, and being able to answer questions about it.

Interviewer: Finally, Kieran, which project do you think will win in the senior category?

Kieran: I'd say there are three clear front runners, and the odds are that the one measuring the amount of bacteria present on various kitchen utensils will come out on top. Of course, I'd rather the project on where fresh cherries deteriorate most slowly won because that's my group's entry, but I don't think it'll happen for them this time. As runner-up, I'd pick the one about whether the quality of our vision is different in the morning and afternoon. Or perhaps the one designed to test the theory that it's best to wear black in hot weather because it is much more efficient than white at absorbing heat from our body – which of course is a much closer energy source than the sun.

Interviewer: You learn something every day! Thank you, Kieran.

Compact Advanced by Peter May ©Cambridge University Press and UCLES 2014

Unit 10, Listening, Part 4

Speaker 1

I seem to spend most of my time defending motorists charged with minor offences instead of fighting for justice for genuine victims of society, as I'd somewhat naively imagined myself doing when I originally applied for this position. But I'd rather be doing that than dealing with paperwork nine-to-five every day because I'm a people person at heart. I'm not one of those over-confident types who starts conversations with everyone in sight, but I do like to chat, and down at the Magistrates court I get to meet clients, witnesses and reporters from the local paper. The salary's not bad, though contrary to the image lawyers sometimes have, that wasn't why I decided to become one.

Speaker 2

I must admit I rarely look ahead in financial terms. I tend to assume I'll either make a loss or at best break even, so usually I end up being pleasantly surprised when neither happens. Not that I ever seriously thought I'd earn more than a basic living when I took this place over from my parents. And I know I should move into bigger premises, but with the unpredictable way the property market has been behaving it would be just my luck to buy just before prices collapsed again, and people cut back on their spending, too. In an ideal world, salaries would go up every year, but that isn't going to happen, is it?

Speaker 3

We're currently in opposition, but there's still plenty to do and meetings until all hours with colleagues. Some of them have very strong views and ideals, and that's fine, but I like to think I'm willing to listen to a wide range of opinions. Actually, I'm going to move on after the next election. It was only ever my intention to spend a few years in the corridors of power before returning to university and applying what I've learnt about politics to some research I want to do. I did both my degrees in business studies and my aim is to compare approaches to management in the political and business spheres. I'm still not sure what I'll do after that.

Speaker 4

Everyone expected me to go into the family business, but even though I left school with pretty good grades there was only ever one thing I wanted to do. Which is this. Not for the material benefits or the lifestyle, but so I could prove to myself that I can actually compete at this level. I may not be quite as gifted as some, so I try to make up for it by putting in as much time and effort as I can on the training ground to perfect my skills. Next weekend, we've got an away game that some of my team mates expect to lose, though I'm a little more optimistic about it.

Speaker 5

I've got a degree in politics so I love covering political stories, especially when a general election is close and the candidates are desperately trying to use us to get their message across to the public. One of my colleagues later went on to become a successful politician himself, a minister in fact. And I must admit that kind of appeals to me, too, so I'm making as many contacts as I can. It'd certainly be an improvement on what I'm currently doing, which consists of working nine-to-five drafting copy on the private lives of celebrities rather than writing anything original or imaginative, which was what initially attracted me to journalism.

Progress test 1 Units 1–2

1 <u>Underline</u> the correct alternatives in this television news report.

The storm began yesterday evening, and by 9 o'clock this morning it **(1)** *had been raining / was raining* continuously for fifteen hours. At 11 o'clock, the local environment agency **(2)** *had issued / issued* a warning to residents living in the town. The water level, it said, **(3)** *rose / was rising* rapidly, with a serious risk of extensive flooding. Unfortunately, by the time most people received the warning, the river **(4)** *has already broken / had already broken* its banks, water **(5)** *flowed / was flowing* into the streets at an alarming rate, and it was too late for the residents to get away.

It's now five o'clock, and **(6)** *I'm standing / I stand* on a hill looking out over the town, which as you can see is a scene of complete devastation. For the last few hours, emergency services **(7)** *have rescued / have been rescuing* residents from their flooded homes, and a spokesperson assures me that within a few hours they **(8)** *will be getting / will have got* everyone out. Happily, on this occasion, there **(9)** *has been / had been* no loss of life, but the damage to local property is immense, and there is no doubt that the clean-up operation **(10)** *is taking / will take* a long time.

This is Rebecca Carlson, reporting for CBT News 24.

2 Complete the sentences with the correct forms of the words in the box. There are two words that you do not need to use.

> broadcast   cover   feature   perform   present
> promote   publish   report   research   schedule

1 The programme was .... for nine o'clock, but didn't begin until 9.30.
2 We now go live to our .... Tricia Bonneville, who is waiting outside the palace with the latest updates.
3 Many viewers complained that the programme was a .... for the singer's new album rather than a documentary about her career.
4 The article contained a lot of factual errors, suggesting that the subject hadn't been well-............................ .
5 And now on BBC1 here is the news, ... by Hitesh Popatlal.
6 .... the story from several different angles, the article was a thoroughly professional piece of journalism.
7 The programme .... interviews with the artist's friends and families, but it wasn't very interesting or informative.
8 The documentary about the group was followed by one of their live .... from the Royal Albert Hall.

3 Complete the extract from a radio interview with **eight** of the words or phrases in the box.

> assist   attend   brought up   economic   economical
> grew up   imply   infer   laying   lying   occasions
> opportunities   raise   rise   sensible   sensitive

Interviewer: So, Pushpa, I understand that you spent your childhood in Birmingham.

Pushpa: That's right. I lived in a small terraced house near the city centre.

Interviewer: Where, I understand, you were **(1)** .... by your grandparents.

Pushpa: Yes. My parents worked for an overseas aid agency and had to move around a lot, so it would have been impractical for them to take me with them. And apart from occasional holidays, we didn't get many **(2)** .... to spend time together.

Interviewer: In your book, you **(3)** .... that you didn't have a very happy childhood.

Pushpa: Well, I wasn't unhappy, exactly, but I was a very **(4)** .... child, you know, little things upset me easily. And my grandparents never had much money. In fact, during the **(5)** .... crisis of the early nineties, life was quite tough, even with the money my parents sent back to us.

Interviewer: But then things changed.

Pushpa: They did. I was sixteen, and I was **(6)** .... in bed one winter's night, freezing cold because my grandparents couldn't afford to put the heating on when I thought I should do something to help.

Interviewer: So, you started looking for work?

Pushpa: Well, I already had a weekend job in a shop, but it paid very little. And my requests to the manager to **(7)** .... my hourly wage had been completely ignored, so I decided to give something else a try.

Interviewer: Which is when you saw an advertisement for a job in the local newspaper office.

Pushpa: Right. So I wrote to them, and much to my surprise, I was asked to **(8)** .... an interview. Which I did, and I got the job.

Interviewer: The job being?

Pushpa: They wanted someone to report on local events, someone who knew the city well ...

Compact Advanced by Peter May ©Cambridge University Press and UCLES 2014   **Photocopiable**

4 Complete this extract from a report by underlining the best word in *italics*.

Cassington Castle Visitors' Centre

This report **(1)** *suggests / outlines / aims / recommends* to look at ways we can improve the visitors' centre at Cassington Castle.

The **(2)** *reason / aims / point / purpose* of the centre is to welcome visitors to the castle and provide them with background information before they visit the castle itself. However, when the centre first opened last year, feedback from visitors was not positive, with several problems being highlighted. The main complaint was that there were always long queues to get into the centre. At the time, we believed that the best **(3)** *way / course / approach / option* of action would be to employ more staff, who could guide visitors through the centre at a controlled pace. Since then, queues and waiting times have been reduced by half, and we have had far fewer complaints. In **(4)** *summary / short / balance / sum*, the situation has greatly improved.

On **(5)** *general / overall / whole / balance*, however, we feel that more improvements could be made as visitors should not need to queue at all to get into the centre. One possible **(6)** *solution / remedy / cure / key* would be to issue timed tickets. These would enable us to control the number of visitors at any one time. We could also **(7)** *think / imagine / regard / consider* issuing visitors with audio guides, which would help to control the speed at which they move through the centre. Furthermore, I strongly **(8)** *mention / present / recommend / consider* an on-line booking system, so that visitors can book their visit in advance.

---

5 Add these prefixes to the words in the sentences. There are three prefixes that you do not need to use.

anti bi de dis en il im mis
out over under

1 Exact visitor numbers to the town are
   (a) ....precise, but we do know that tourists
   (b) ....number locals during the peak season.

2 I'm reasonably fluent in Spanish, but I think it would be a bit **(a)** ....honest to describe myself as **(b)** ....lingual.

3 With limited accommodation available, we need to
   (a) ....sure that the town doesn't become too
   (b) ....crowded during the summer.

4 The newspaper article **(a)** ....led its readers into thinking that **(b)** ....social behaviour was a major problem in the town at the weekends.

6 Complete passage B so that it has the same meaning as passage A. In each space, use a present, past or perfect participle, and any other words which are necessary.

A A few years ago, I did a teacher training course in my home city, Tunis, which prepared me to teach Arabic to overseas students. I worked hard, and I got a good grade at the end.
I knew that I wanted to work abroad, but as I didn't know where I wanted to go exactly, I started looking in the career sections of various online newspapers around the world. But then I came across an international teachers' website which listed teaching vacancies around the world. One of these was for an Arabic teacher at an international language school in London. The school was located near Trafalgar Square in the city centre, and specialised in teaching languages to business people who were going to work abroad. I decided to apply for the post, since I had not only the right qualifications for the job, but also some relatives living in the city. They had lived there for several years, so would be familiar with the city and would be able to help me find my feet. As I had never been to London before, I decided it would be good to have someone to turn to for help and support.

B A few years ago, I did a teacher training course in my home city, Tunis, which prepared me to teach Arabic to overseas students. **(1)** .... hard, I got a good grade at the end.
(2) .... that I wanted to work abroad, but **(3)** .... where I wanted to go exactly, I started looking in the career sections of various online newspapers around the world. But then I came across an international teachers' website **(4)** .... teaching vacancies around the world. One of these was for an Arabic teacher at an international language school in London.
(5) .... near Trafalgar Square in the city centre, the school specialised in teaching languages to business people who were going to work abroad. I decided to apply for the post, **(6)** .... not only the right qualifications for the job, but also some relatives living in the city. **(7)** .... there for several years, they would be familiar with the city and would be able to help me find my feet. **(8)** .... to London before, I decided it would be good to have someone to turn to for help and support.

Progress test 2 Units 3–4

1 Complete the second sentence so that it has a similar meaning to the first sentence. Use <u>four</u> words only in each gap.

1. a) "I'll help you with your homework over the weekend," I said to Karl.
   b) I told Karl that .... with his homework over the weekend.

2. a) Mario rang me from Australia last week and said, "I'm having fun here with my family."
   b) Mario rang me from Australia last week and said that he .... with his family.

3. a) "Let's go out for dinner on Saturday," said Petra.
   b) Petra suggested .... on Saturday.

4. a) Mustafa said, "I didn't do any revision for the exam."
   b) Mustafa admitted .... for the exam.

5. a) "Can you tell me where the station is?" asked the man in the suit.
   b) The man in the suit asked me .... him where the station was.

6. a) Sandra said to me, "I'm sorry I didn't call you at the weekend."
   b) Sandra apologised .... at the weekend.

7. a) The instructions said, "Don't open the unit without disconnecting the power supply first."
   b) The instructions warned users .... unit without disconnecting the power supply first.

8. a) "I'll lend you the money for a new camera," Nadine said to me.
   b) Nadine offered .... money for a new camera.

9. a) "Don't forget to call your mother when you get home," said Joti.
   b) Joti reminded .... mother when I got home.

10. a) "I didn't take any money from your wallet," said Jon angrily.
    b) Jon angrily denied .... my wallet.

2 Complete the gaps in the text with one word from the first box and one word from the second box. You should use each word from the first box once only.

| close dysfunctional extended fair-weather living nuclear school stormy |

| family friend parents relationship relatives |

I come from a typically 'western' **(1)** .... , with me, my parents and my two sisters living together in a small terraced house in the suburbs. We all get on well and do lots of things together. However, having said that, I do have a rather **(2)** .... with my younger sister, Alicia. We're always arguing and disagreeing about things. However, our arguments never last long, and they are never that serious.

The person who is closest to me outside my family is my old **(3)** .... Francis. We first met when we were at kindergarten, and have enjoyed a **(4)** .... ever since. He comes from a rather **(5)** .... They all lead separate lives, and his younger brother is always getting into trouble. Outside his immediate family, his only **(6)** .... are his uncle Ted and auntie Fay, who live a few streets away. Francis gets on much better with them, and spends more time with them than he does with his mother and father. In fact, I'm surprised he doesn't just move in with them and make it official!

When Francis isn't around, I often spend time with Mangal. I like him a lot, but he's a bit of a **(7)** .... He's fine when things are going well for me, but if I have a problem, he'll keep his distance. Mangal lives in a large house with his **(8)** .... , that is, his parents, grandparents, brothers, sisters and an aunt and uncle or two. I love going round there, as their house is always so noisy and full of life.

3 <u>Underline</u> the correct word in *italics* in these dialogues to make idioms with *keep*.

1. A: I'm taking my driving test tomorrow.
   B: Good luck. I'll be keeping my *legs / eyes / fingers / arms* crossed for you.

2. A: You must have been furious when Alice broke your new camera.
   B: Well, I was rather annoyed, but I managed to keep my *quiet / cool / calm / peace*.

3 A: Did Martin arrange a job interview for you at his company like he promised?

   B: Yes, he kept his *word / truth / honesty / say*, although I never expected he would.

4 A: I'm going to the rock festival at the weekend.

   B: Me too. I'll keep *an ear / a check / a search / an eye* out for you.

5 A: People are saying that they haven't seen you at the club recently.

   B: Well, to be honest, I'm trying to keep a *reduced / low / little / hidden* profile at the moment.

6 A: It was really funny when our teacher couldn't stop sneezing in class.

   B: I know. I tried not to smile, but I just couldn't keep a straight *head / mouth / face / look*.

7 A: Do you know what time you'll get to my place tomorrow?

   B: Not yet. It depends on the trains. I'll keep you *alerted / posted / warned / detailed*.

8 A: What's your sister doing for work these days?

   B: I'm not sure. She's had so many jobs that I find it hard to keep *path / route / track / lane* of what she's doing.

4 Complete the gaps in these two paragraphs with a passive form of the verbs in brackets.

Paragraph A
My parents' house is currently on the market. The sale **(1)** .... (arrange) by an estate agent who promises that they won't charge any fees if a buyer **(2)** .... (not / find) by the end of the year. A lot of people have viewed the house, and the estate agent is confident that a sale **(3)** .... (make) in the next month or so. The house **(4)** .... (must / sell) by September, as that is when my parents move into their new home.

Paragraph B
Things are not going well for the mobile phone supplier Talkbox. The firm **(5)** .... (report / make) a loss of almost £6 million in the last twelve months. This might have something to do with the fact that in April they **(6)** .... (take over) by the telecommunications giant GoTel, who even back then **(7)** .... (know) by many in the telecommunications business to be struggling financially. These people believe that the company **(8)** .... (force) to cease trading within six months unless they start making a profit very soon.

5 Complete the passage with the correct form of the verbs in the box to make phrasal verbs with *out*. There are two verbs that you do not need to use.

back	bail	check	chill	cut	get	kick
run	splash	start				

In the evenings I usually **(1)** .... out at home in front of the television, but occasionally I like to go into town and **(2)** .... out on a really good meal. In fact, last night I **(3)** .... out a new vegetarian restaurant in the town centre. I must say that I thought it was really good. The owners **(4)** .... out with a small stall at the market selling cooked food to shoppers, but they were so successful that they soon had enough money to open a proper restaurant. Unfortunately, business was slow at first, and a couple of people who had invested in the restaurant **(5)** .... out. Eventually, the restaurant owners started to **(6)** .... out of money and the bank refused to **(7)** .... them out. Then they had a bit of good luck. A famous film star turned up for dinner and praised the owners for the quality of their food. The story soon **(8)** .... out, and business suddenly started to pick up. Now it's almost impossible to get a table unless you book days in advance.

6 Choose the best options to complete this passage.

I lost my job a few months ago when the company I worked for, which had been in trouble for a while, was forced to close down **(1)** *for a start / for good*. I received a small final payment from the company by way of compensation, but the money soon went.
(2) *First and foremost / For a start* there was my rent, which immediately used up a third of the money. Then there were all the other expenses that day-to-day living requires, such as food and electricity. Within a few weeks, my bank account was empty.

Now, **(3)** *let alone / other than* the cash I receive for occasional part-time work, I have very little money coming in. It's hard to get by on such a small income, but **(4)** *by and large / other than* I manage. One thing I have to do is to decide where my priorities lie with regard to how I spend my money. **(5)** *For the time being / With a view to* window shopping is all I can afford!

Last night I sat and made myself a plan for the future. **(6)** *First and foremost / For good*, I have to find a new job. I have decided to go to the library daily **(7)** *with a view to / by and large* searching for a post by using the computers and newspapers available there. At the moment, I can hardly afford to buy food **(8)** *other than / let alone* a daily newspaper so the library will be a great help to me.

Progress test 3 Units 5–6

1 Complete each gap in these conditional sentences with one word from the box. Use each word once only.

> assuming condition had long provided should
> supposing were

1 You'll lose weight, but only on .... that you stick to a calorie-controlled diet.

2 .... you eaten less last night, you wouldn't have had such a bad night's sleep.

3 .... you needed medical treatment while abroad, what would you do?

4 You would feel much healthier than you do now .... you to take more exercise.

5 .... the weather is nice tomorrow, let's meet up for a round of golf.

6 You'll recover quickly as .... as you follow your doctor's advice.

7 .... you react badly to the medicine, contact your doctor as soon as possible.

8 .... that everything goes to plan, we should arrive between three and four o'clock.

2 Complete these paragraphs with the correct forms of the word in *italics*.

1 *prevent*

Many people look on vitamin tablets as a form of .... medicine. In other words, they believe these tablets are a way of .... , or at least reducing the risk of, certain illnesses.

2 *medicine*

Some jobs require a doctor's statement to say that you are .... fit for work. Pilots, for example, have to go for regular .... check-ups to ensure they can continue to fly safely.

3 *surgery*

The earthquake has caused thousands of serious injuries, and doctors and .... at the scene of the disaster are urgently requesting medicines and .... supplies.

4 *treat*

Several courses of .... are available for tackling the virus, but .... everyone affected is going to take a long time and cost a lot of money.

5 *clinic*

The drug was put through several .... trials, and was then distributed to several doctors and .... who tested it on their patients and reported on its effectiveness.

3 Complete these sentences with an infinitive or *-ing* form of the verb in brackets, adding *to* where necessary. In some cases, more than one answer is possible.

1 I usually avoid .... (go) into town at the weekend.

2 The art exhibition inspired me .... (take up) painting.

3 Every night we can hear the man next door .... (play) the violin.

4 Janet suggested .... (visit) the new art gallery in the town centre.

5 My parents never let me .... (go) out during the week.

6 I must confess that I love .... (listen) to jazz and blues when I'm on my own.

7 I persuaded Helen .... (come) to the show with me.

8 After five hours on our feet, we started .... (feel) a bit tired.

4 Complete each sentence in these pairs with the correct form of the verb in italics (*-ing or to* + infinitive)

1 *call*

I meant .... you yesterday, but I ran out of time.

Getting tickets for the show meant .... an automated ticket seller.

2 *say*

I regret .... the concert was terrible, especially as the conductor was standing behind me when I did!

We regret .... that all tickets for tonight's show have sold out.

3 *buy*

I remembered .... sugar and milk, but I'm afraid I didn't get any tea.

I know I have tickets for tonight's show, because I clearly remember .... them on-line when they went on sale.

4 *drop*

I'll never forget .... my cousin's new camera, and the horrified look on her face as it hit the ground.

Don't forget .... off those books at the library when you go into town.

5 *talk*

The speaker went on .... despite continual interruptions from the audience.

After explaining how the group was formed, the singer went on .... about his first album.

5 Choose which word (**A, B, C** or **D**) best fits each gap in these sentences.

1 The museum has .... a reward of £10,000 to anyone finding and returning the stolen painting.

   A awarded **B** donated **C** granted **D** offered

2 We walked through the gallery .... in admiration at all of the wonderful pictures.

   A gazing **B** glancing **C** glimpsing **D** viewing

3 I've recently re-read Jonathan Swift's .... novel Gulliver's Travels, first published in 1726.

   A antique **B** classic **C** classical **D** obsolete

4 The artist .... the different techniques he had used to create the painting.

   A demonstrated **B** exhibited **C** interpreted **D** performed

5 Exams are not the best way of .... an art student's ability.

   A appreciating **B** assessing **C** estimating **D** evaluating

6 The government is .... £20 million of this year's budget for a new arts centre in the city.

   A allocating **B** assigning **C** devoting **D** distributing

7 The audience at the show was .... largely of young people.

   A assembled **B** built **C** composed **D** manufactured

8 A lot of important .... documents were destroyed when the library burnt down.

   A elderly **B** historic **C** historical **D** outdated

6 Complete this conversation by filling each gap with an appropriate adjective from the box, and then <u>underlining</u> which adverb in *italics* best collocates with that adjective.

> acclaimed hilarious imaginative overrated talented tedious

Tom: How did you enjoy the film last night?

Emma: I thought it was brilliant – much better than I expected.

Tom: In what way?

Emma: Well, I'm not a big fan of the director. I know people are always saying how brilliant his films are, but I've always found them (**1**) *dreadfully / eagerly* .... What I mean is, they're not bad but they're definitely not as good as everyone says they are. And although people say he is (**2**) *absolutely / wonderfully* .... , I don't think he's any more gifted than all of the other film makers out there.

Tom: What about his second film, the one that was based on that (**3**) *totally / widely* .... bestselling novel, er, what was it called?

Emma: 'Forward he cried.'

Tom: That's the one. I thought that was quite good.

Emma: Well, I didn't. I thought everything about it was awful. The acting, the camera work, the soundtrack. A five-year-old could have done a better job. And it was (**4**) *absolutely / dreadfully* .... as well. It was so boring that I even fell asleep at one point.

Tom: Oh dear. So why did you go to see his latest film?

Emma: Well, it was a departure from the sort of thing he usually does. I mean, he's never done comedy before.

Tom: And you enjoyed it.

Emma: Oh yes, it was (**5**) *absolutely / deeply* .... I haven't laughed so much for ages. And the story was (**6**) *perfectly / wonderfully* .... There were lots of clever, original ideas that really made it something special.

Progress test 4 Units 7–8

1 Complete each gap in B with <u>two</u> words from the box, so that the meaning is the same as A.

> at before did do else Little Never no no No not nowhere on only only Seldom sooner there under when

A I love living in London, my home city. It's noisy and overcrowded, but there isn't such a large variety of things to do anywhere else in the world. I seldom leave the city, and I wouldn't normally consider spending much time in the countryside under any circumstances. However, when an old friend unexpectedly rang me and invited me to stay at his house in rural Oxfordshire for a few days, I decided to go. It had been a long, hot summer, and I was fed up with the continuous heat and crowds of people everywhere. I didn't really realise how much my life was about to change.

The next day, I took a train from Paddington station to Oxford. As soon as the train left the suburbs and started heading out into the countryside, my spirits began to lift. From Oxford, I caught a bus to the village of Hamley Crossing, where my friend lived. However, I didn't get that far. A few miles out of Oxford, the bus stopped to pick up some passengers. I glanced out of the window and saw, on a hillside overlooking the countryside, a small cottage. It was surrounded by trees and fields, and looked really peaceful and welcoming. I had never seen such a beautiful place before.

I must have been under some sort of hypnotic spell, because I didn't realise that I had got off the bus and was walking towards the cottage until I heard the sound of birds singing and felt the breeze in my hair. It was as if I was being magically drawn to the place. I absolutely had to see it close up, and I didn't consider the fact that my friend would be waiting for me in Hamley Crossing.

B I love living in London, my home city. It's noisy and overcrowded, but (1) .... in the world is there such a large variety of things to do. (2) .... I leave the city, and normally, (3) .... circumstances would I consider spending much time in the countryside. However, when an old friend unexpectedly rang me and invited me to stay at his house in rural Oxfordshire for a few days, I decided to go. It had been a long, hot summer, and (4) .... was I fed up with the continuous heat, but also with the crowds of people everywhere. (5) .... I realise how much my life was about to change.

The next day, I took a train from Paddington station to Oxford. (6) .... had the train left the suburbs and started heading out into the countryside than my spirits began to lift. From Oxford, I caught a bus to the village of Hamley Crossing, where my friend lived. However, I didn't get that far. A few miles out of Oxford, the bus stopped to pick up some passengers. I glanced out of the window and (7) .... a hillside overlooking the countryside stood a small cottage. It was surrounded by trees and fields, and looked really peaceful and welcoming. (8) .... had I seen such a beautiful place.

I must have been under some sort of hypnotic spell, because (9) .... I heard the sound of birds singing and felt the breeze in my hair did I realise that I had got off the bus and was walking towards the cottage. It was as if I was being magically drawn to the place. I absolutely had to see it close up, and (10) .... time did I consider my friend who would be waiting to meet me in Hamley Crossing.

2 Complete the idioms in these sentences by underlining the correct word in *italics*.

1 I hadn't heard from Sharif for years, and then this morning, completely out of the *blue / red / green / black*, he telephoned and said he would be in the country next week.

2 I think that by secretly passing information to one of your company's competitors, you're playing with *earth / fire / water / wind*.

3 Your ideas are wonderful in theory, but in all honesty they're impractical and not very down to *earth / floor / land / ground*.

4 As you can imagine, when I passed my driving test I was absolutely over the *edge / moon / sun / top*.

5 When it comes to saving the environment, recycling paper is just a drop in the *lake / ocean / river / sea*.

6 The speaker's ideas about how we can all help the environment were original, interesting and a real breath of fresh *air / ideas / oxygen / wind*.

7 The sudden disappearance of bees from our gardens is just the *end / point / tip / top* of the iceberg; there are many more environmental problems that we aren't aware of yet.

3 Arrange the letters in **bold** to make adverbs. The first letter of each word is in its correct place.

1 The fire destroyed hundreds of acres of woodland, but **fnreytuloat** .... nobody was hurt.

2 **Aryepnpatl** .... a lot of household waste that we think goes to recycling gets burned or buried instead.

3 I don't think that electric vehicles are very good, although **amtdedlyit** .... I've never driven one.

4 Domestic solar panels can help reduce the amount of fossil fuels we use, but **gaerlelyn** .... I think their benefits are minimal.

5 I thought the lecture on alternative power would be rather dull, but **utednxpelecy** .... it was absolutely fascinating.

6 An unusual, very colourful plant has **mtoruisyslye** .... appeared in my back garden.

7 **Uynrinulgsprsi** ...., countries that do little to reduce pollution have some of the worst environmental problems.

8 I don't know what we can do to reduce pollution, but **ooislybuv** .... something has to be done as soon as possible.

4 Complete each gap in this review with <u>one</u> or <u>two</u> words only.

One of my favourite books is called *The Education of Hyman Kaplan*, a collection of short stories **(1)** .... are set in an English class at a New York night school. Each story centres around a single lesson, and in particular around a student called Hyman Kaplan, **(2)** .... determined efforts to learn and speak English confuse and frustrate his teacher, Mr Parkhill, and the students **(3)** .... he studies. The author Leo Rosten, **(4)** .... wrote books and magazine articles on subjects as diverse as politics, sociology and art, based the stories on his own experiences as a teacher at a night school in Chicago, **(5)** .... he taught English in the 1930s.

What I like about this book is its gentle humour, the clever use of language, and the way the characters, **(6)** .... come from all over the world, are so wonderfully portrayed without being stereotyped. Hyman Kaplan, **(7)** .... we know very little except for the fact that he recently emigrated from Europe, is a loud, colourful and larger-than-life character. He frequently misunderstands things, but he tries hard and he always has an answer to any question that Mr Parkhill asks, none **(8)** .... are correct. For example, during a lesson **(9)** .... the class is learning about abstract nouns, he gives the opposite of 'dismay' as 'next June'. Each lesson usually ends in chaos, with Hyman Kaplan completely unaware that he is the cause of it.

The Education of Hyman Kaplan is a book **(10)** .... I frequently turn to when I want to switch off and relax. It is a perfect example of what people call 'comfort reading', and I would not hesitate to recommend it.

5 Complete the gaps in this passage with the correct form of the words in brackets. In each case, you should add a prefix and a suffix, making any other changes to the spelling.

The pollution coming from the construction site opposite our school was absolutely **(1)** .... (describe). Sometimes, the air was so thick with diesel fumes and dust, it was difficult to breathe. And you just couldn't get away from the noise. You could hear it wherever you went, even in the classrooms furthest from the site.

The principal wrote a letter to the local council, who were responsible for the site, expressing her **(2)** .... (approve). In return they sent her a rather **(3)** .... (person) letter, one that they clearly sent out to anyone who made a complaint. The letter simply said that essential building work was being carried out, and any pollution or noise was being kept to a minimum.

The principal wrote a second letter to them, clearly stating her **(4)** .... (satisfy) with their reply. She also said that she believed they were acting **(5)** .... (legal), as no measures seemed to have been put in place to protect her students and staff (and general members of the public) from the noise and pollution. This time she received a really rude reply, saying she was making a big fuss over an **(6)** .... (signify) matter, and accusing her of being both **(7)** .... (profession) and **(8)** .... (protect) towards her students!

6 Complete the sentences with the correct forms of the words in the box.

broad   deep   detain   maintain   prove   resolve   strong

1 Last January, the river froze to a .... of over a metre.

2 I've made a few New Year ...., one of which is to start looking for a new job.

3 I've always believed that admitting you've made a mistake is a sign of ....

4 The hotel employs a .... team who are on call 24 hours a day if there are any problems.

5 I walked the length and .... of the High Street looking for my mobile phone, which I had lost earlier.

6 There's absolutely no .... that the money was stolen.

7 There have been some concerns that people charged with crimes are being held in .... for too long without a trial.

Progress test 5 Units 9–10

1 Complete the sentences with a word or phrase from A, the correct form of a verb from B, and any other words that are necessary. In some cases more than one answer is possible.

A able to   can   could   couldn't   have to
   might   must   need to   should

B be (x2)   do   go   see   steal   stop   take

1 I wasn't impressed by the talk on alternative energy. It .... really interesting, but I thought it was rather boring.

2 I managed to finish my project on time, but I .... it without your help, so thank you very much for everything you did.

3 The fire in the laboratory caused a lot of damage, but at least we .... it spreading to the rest of the building.

4 I can't find my wallet anywhere. It .... I can't think of any other explanation.

5 I .... to the conference yesterday because it was cancelled, so I stayed at home.

6 I have some really exciting news that .... of interest to you.

7 These pills that the doctor gave me for my throat infection are supposed to be very effective, but I'll .... them for at least a week before they begin to work.

8 It's sometimes said that the Great Wall of China is the only man-made structure that .... from space.

2 Decide if the word in **bold** in each of these sentences is being used correctly. If not, replace it with one of the words from the box.

analysis   approach   factor   hypothesis   procedure

1 We have established a set of **criteria** .... to decide whether or not the product has commercial value.

2 Cost will be a major **significance** .... in the development and production of our latest range of telecommunications products.

3 Chemical **deduction** .... of the plant revealed a high level of salicylic acid.

4 I'm not sure what **relevance** .... my age has when it comes to deciding whether or not I can join the course.

5 So far she has failed to convince him of the benefits of regular exercise, so she has decided to take a different **method** ....

6 We can't accurately predict the outcome of the experiment because of all the **variables** .... that are involved.

7 In the interests of health and safety, students must follow the correct **principle** .... in the laboratory at all times.

8 We don't know why people who eat lots of hot chillies rarely get colds, but one **concept** .... suggests it is because of their high vitamin C content.

3 Complete the sentences with the prepositions in the box. You can use some prepositions twice, but there is one preposition you do not need.

about   against   by   for   of   to   with

1 The results from the experiment were consistent .... those obtained in earlier research.

2 The research clinic is adjacent .... the hospital.

3 Access to the database is restricted .... senior research staff only.

4 The company was highly prejudiced .... employing anyone over 40.

5 Plants which are deprived .... their recommended amount of light will still grow, but at a greatly reduced rate.

6 We have just found out that our project is eligible .... a government grant.

7 The article was supposed to be objective, but it was heavily biased .... council policy.

8 I felt frustrated .... her continual refusal to accept my way of doing things.

4 Underline the correct word or phrase in *italics* in **(a)** and the correct word or phrase in **(b)** in these sentences. In two cases, both options are possible.

1 I didn't get a good grade in my exam, and really **(a)** *hope / wish* I **(b)** *had spent / have spend* more time revising for it.

2 Travelling around Europe last summer was alright, but I'd **(a)** *rather / prefer* **(b)** *go / have gone* to the USA instead.

3 You're a rather pessimistic person, and I think it's **(a)** *about time / high time* you **(b)** *start / started* taking a more positive approach to life.

4 I'd **(a)** *prefer / rather* you **(b)** *didn't tell / won't tell* anyone that I'm taking my driving test tomorrow.

5 I'm finding it really hard to get any work done today. **(a)** *If just / If only* people **(b)** *will stop / would stop* interrupting me all the time.

6 It's difficult to talk with all this noise, so I'd **(a)** *prefer / rather* it if we **(b)** *could go / went* somewhere a little quieter.

5 Complete the second sentence in each pair so that it has a similar meaning to the first sentence, using a verb from A and <u>two</u> particles from B. You do not need to use all the particles.

A: brush   check   come   get   look   put   read   stand

B: against   back   of   on   out   round   to   up   with

1 Mara seemed upset at school today, so I'll call later and make sure she's alright.

Mara seemed upset at school today, so I'll call later and .... her.

2 There aren't many people I respect, but my uncle Jamal is one of them.

There aren't many people I ...., but my uncle Jamal is one of them.

3 I'm going to Rome next week, so I'd better practise my Italian.

I'm going to Rome next week, so I'd better .... my Italian.

4 Whenever I visit another country for the first time, I try to learn something about it before I go.

Whenever I visit another country for the first time, I try to .... it before I go.

5 This week I hope that I'll finally start doing some revision.

This week I hope that I'll .... doing some revision.

6 I refuse to tolerate my neighbour's loud music any longer.

I refuse to .... my neighbour's loud music any longer.

7 I'm not afraid to defend myself against people who try to push me around.

I'm not afraid to .... people who try to push me around.

8 I enjoy the challenge when I have to deal with unexpected problems at work.

I enjoy the challenge when I .... unexpected problems at work.

6 Read these paragraphs, and match two adjectives with each person. One adjective is not needed.

> anti-social   conscientious   courageous   idealistic   imaginative   insecure   insensitive   modest   naïve   narrow-minded   outgoing   talkative   well-balanced

1 Pierre   .... I love meeting new people and getting involved in things, and everyone agrees that I'm the life and soul of any party. On the other hand, I am often accused of failing to take people's feelings into consideration.

2 Nadine   ....
As a writer, it helps that I'm good at coming up with ideas that are interesting and unusual. However, I'm not a very confident person and am often uncertain about my own abilities or whether people will like my books.

3 Stefan   ....
I guess I'm a calm and reasonable person, and usually show good judgement. Unfortunately, I also have the unfortunate habit of believing everything people tell me, or that their intentions are good.

4 Akiko   ....
I usually get good grades in my college work. That's not because I'm particularly intelligent but because I put a lot of effort into everything I do. I prefer my own company to that of others and spend a lot of time on my own.

5 Carol   ....
People are often coming up to me and saying things like 'Hey, I loved your latest film'. My usual response is 'Thank you, you're too kind'. I don't like to be seen as a great film director, just an ordinary woman doing her job. I'm always happy to chat about my films, however. In fact, I'm happy to chat about anything.

6 Charles   ....
I believe very strongly that there are no problems in the world that can't be solved by people getting together and looking for solutions. Also I have very little time for anyone whose ideas differ from mine.

Progress tests answer key

Each Progress Test has 50 marks so you can easily work out students' percentage scores.

Progress Test 1

1 1 had been raining   2 issued   3 was rising
4 had already broken   5 was flowing   6 I'm standing
7 have been rescuing   8 will have got   9 has been
10 will take

2 1 scheduled   2 reporter   3 promotion   4 researched
5 presented   6 Covering   7 featured   8 performances
Broadcast and *publish* are not needed.

3 1 brought up   2 opportunities   3 imply   4 sensitive
5 economic   6 lying   7 raise   8 attend

4 1 aims   2 purpose   3 course   4 short   5 balance
6 solution   7 consider   8 recommend

5 1 (a) im   (b) out   2 (a) dis   (b) bi
3 (a) en   (b) over   4 (a) mis   (b) anti
de, il and *under* are not needed.

6 1 Having worked   2 Knowing   3 not knowing
4 listing   5 Located   6 having   7 Having lived
8 Never having been / Not having been

Progress Test 2

1 1 I would help him   2 was having fun there   3 going
out for dinner   4 not doing any revision   5 if / whether I
could tell   6 for not calling me   7 not to open the
8 to lend me the   9 me to call my   10 taking any money
from

2 1 nuclear family   2 stormy relationship   3 school friend
4 close relationship   5 dysfunctional family
6 living relatives   7 fair-weather friend   8 extended family

3 1 fingers   2 cool   3 word   4 an eye   5 low   6 face
7 posted   8 track

4 1 is being arranged   2 hasn't / has not been found / isn't /
is not found   3 will be made   4 must be sold
5 is reported to have made   6 were taken over   7 were /
was known   8 will be forced

5 1 chill   2 splash   3 checked   4 started   5 backed
6 run   7 bail   8 got   *Cut* and *kick* are not needed.

6 1 for good   2 For a start   3 other than   4 by and
large   5 For the time being   6 First and foremost
7 with a view to   8 let alone

Compact Advanced by Peter May ©Cambridge University Press and UCLES 2014   **Photocopiable**

Progress Test 3

1 1 condition   2 Had   3 Supposing   4 were
5 Assuming / Provided   6 long   7 Should
8 Provided / Assuming

2 1 preventative; preventing   2 medically; medical
3 surgeons; surgical   4 treatment; treating
5 clinical; clinicians

3 1 going   2 to take up   3 playing   4 visiting   5 go
6 listening / to listen   7 to come   8 feeling / to feel

4 1 to call; calling   2 saying; to say   3 to buy; buying
4 dropping; to drop   5 talking; to talk

5 1 D   2 A   3 B   4 A   5 B   6 A   7 C   8 C

6 1 dreadfully overrated   2 wonderfully talented
3 widely acclaimed   4 dreadfully tedious   5 absolutely
hilarious   6 wonderfully imaginative

Progress Test 4

1 1 nowhere else   2 Seldom do   3 under no
4 not only   5 Little did   6 No sooner   7 there on
8 Never before   9 only when   10 at no

2 1 blue   2 fire   3 earth   4 moon   5 ocean   6 air
7 tip

3 1 fortunately   2 Apparently   3 admittedly
4 generally   5 unexpectedly   6 mysteriously
7 Unsurprisingly   8 obviously

4 1 which / that   2 whose   3 with whom   4 who
5 where / in which / at which   6 who   7 about whom
8 of which   9 where / in which   10 which

5 1 indescribable   2 disapproval   3 impersonal
4 dissatisfaction   5 illegally   6 insignificant
7 unprofessional   8 overprotective

6 1 depth   2 resolutions   3 strength   4 maintenance
5 breadth   6 proof   7 detention

Progress Test 5

1 1 could have been / should have been   2 couldn't have
done   3 were able to stop   4 must have been stolen
5 didn't need to go   6 might be / should be / could be
7 have to / need to take   8 can be seen

2 1 correct   2 factor   3 analysis   4 correct
5 approach   6 correct   7 procedure   8 hypothesis

3 1 with   2 to   3 to   4 against
5 of   6 for   7 against   8 by

4 1 wish; had spent   2 rather; have gone   3 about time *or*
high time; started   4 rather; didn't tell   5 If only; would
stop   6 prefer / could go *or* went

5 1 check up on   2 look up to   3 brush up on   4 read up on
5 get round to   6 put up with   7 stand up to
8 come up against

6 1 outgoing + insensitive   2 imaginative + insecure
3 well-balanced + naïve   4 conscientious + anti-social
5 modest + talkative   6 idealistic + narrow-minded

None of the speakers could be described as *courageous*,
according to the texts.

Author Acknowledgements

The author and publishers would like to thank **Rawdon Wyatt** for writing the Progress tests and answer keys.
The author would like to thank Judith Greet, Jane Coates and Una Yeung for their input and efficiency.

Corpus

Development of this publication has made use of the Cambridge English Corpus (CEC). The CEC is a computer database of contemporary spoken and written English, which currently stands at over one billion words. It includes British English, American English and other varieties of English. It also includes the Cambridge Learner Corpus, developed in collaboration with Cambridge English Language Assessment. Cambridge University Press has built up the CEC to provide evidence about language use that helps to produce better language teaching materials.

English Profile

This product is informed by the English Vocabulary Profile, built as part of English Profile, a collaborative programme designed to enhance the learning, teaching and assessment of English worldwide. Its main funding partners are Cambridge University Press and Cambridge English Language Assessment and its aim is to create a 'profile' for English linked to the Common European Framework of Reference for Languages (CEF). English Profile outcomes, such as the English Vocabulary Profile, will provide detailed information about the language that learners can be expected to demonstrate at each CEF level, offering a clear benchmark for learners' proficiency. For more information, please visit www.englishprofile.org

Cambridge Dictionaries

Cambridge dictionaries are the world's most widely used dictionaries for learners of English. The dictionaries are available in print and online at dictionary.cambridge.org. Copyright © Cambridge University Press, reproduced with permission.